The Complete Guide to
SNOWDON

To Idris and Tim

I fy nhad a fy mab

The Complete Guide to
SNOWDON

Robert Jones

seren

Seren is the book imprint of
Poetry Wales Press Ltd
Nolton Street, Bridgend, CF31 3AE
www.seren-books.com

First published by Gwasg Carreg Gwalch in 1992
The new edition first published in 2007

ISBN 978-1-85411-421-1

The publisher works with the support of the Welsh Books Council

Printed in Plantin by

Contents

Acknowledgements

Although writing a book is a satisfying task, and takes a great deal of time and effort from the author, what is often not realised by the readers, is the tremendous amount of help given by other people, without which many books would not be published. Such help can be given in many ways, but in the end it is the fact that it was given at all that counts, and most authors use such acknowledgement pages as this to thank their helpers in a way that is not only memorable, but also 'everlasting' – in printed words. I shall be no exception to this act of thanksgiving, and listed below are the people to whom I wish to extend my gratitude.

Many authors forget that their early start in life often makes an important contribution to their literary exploits, but I would like to acknowledge the way in which my late parents (Myfanwy and ldris) and indeed my late grandmother (Mary Anne [Gwalia]), not only taught me to be proud of being Welsh, but made my early days in the south Wales valley town of Rhymney as pleasant and as inspiring as it was for the town's only really famous literary master – Idris Davies.

Living near the Brecon Beacons meant that my early forays into 'mountaineering' were climbing to the top of Corn Ddu or Pen-y-fan, and it was only much later in life that I became enamoured by the scenery of North Wales, and in particular of the summits of Snowdonia. But it is to my friend Phil Booth of Trefriw that I owe so much gratitude for not only introducing me to these mountain ranges, but also to Snowdon. After our first attempt of the 'horseshoe' in thick mist, I was determined to find out as much as possible of the mountain I never actually saw, and over the years, Phil was an unfailing companion on many a walk. Equally, my thanks go to his wife Kath, who was such a superb supplier of packed lunches (and more importantly marvellous dinners after our strenuous days on the massif).

Obtaining the inspiration and collecting the information for a book is one thing, but making sure the facts are correct is another, and my sincere thanks go to the staff of the Snowdonia National Park Authority and the National Trust in Wales for the help they have given ensuring the accuracy of the contents of this updated edition.

Last but by no means least; I must acknowledge my publishers – Seren – who appreciated the need for this second edition after an absence from bookshelves for far too many years.

Thanks to you all.

Robert Jones, 2007

Foreword

Despite having bagged a few summits in Snowdonia, I was in my teens before I managed to ascend Snowdon, via Crib Goch and Crib y Ddysgl. It was a Saturday in July, and we were blessed with good weather. Since that day in the Fifties, I have been able both to marvel at and to despise the massif; to marvel and enjoy nature on a warm day in Summer; to deplore the toll to life that occurs at regular intervals when humans challenge nature head on and fail to read its moods with fatal results.

This book sets out to inform the reader about Snowdon, Yr Wyddfa, and those other lofty satellites which are contained by the valleys of Llanberis, Nangwynant and Cwellyn. Many books have been written about Eryri or Snowdonia, the text of which have included information about the highest mountain in England and Wales, but this is a rare book which has been dedicated to the massif, its many moods, and its many facets. Its history is interlinked with that of the shepherds who have toiled for decades to earn their living from a hostile land; who have produced food for the nation and who by all indications will not be rewarded in future for production, but for helping to maintain the landscape as we know it now.

This book touches on the many aspects of Snowdon which make this such a great mountain. As a reference book, it will in all probability remind its readers of their efforts to gain that summit cairn, whether it was on a blistering day or bowing to a southwesterly gale; that sunrise, sunset or waiting for dawn after an all night search.

Robert Jones has undertaken a great task to amass the facts, from a massif in solitude beneath the ocean to the present mass trespass of human forms. A most informative book dedicated to that most celebrated hill 'Yr Wyddfa'.

John Ellis Roberts M.B.E., March 1992

Preface

Snowdon – Yr Wyddfa – the highest, grandest, and most popular peak in Wales. This book is intended as a guide, not only to the many routes to the summit of this wonderful mountain, but also to its flora, its fauna, its local history, and, above all, to the feel of the atmosphere that exudes from such a great place.It is also a guide to what might happen in the future if we do not look after this unique habitat.

The mountain itself draws some 500,000 visitors to its summit each year. Some arrive there the easy way - by train. The others by one or other of the superb scenic walking tracks. The modern visitor cannot experience Snowdon as it was, with its industries, its old forests, and its eagles, but I hope this book will provide a flavour of what they might have found, even just a hundred years ago. Visitors might also like to ponder the fact that when they stand on the summit, at a height of 3560 feet, this piece of land was, over 400 million years ago, on the seabed of a vast ocean.

To the typical day tourist, Snowdon is a place where they can visit in the relative comfort of a unique train journey, and see wonderful views (on a good day!). To others, it's just another mountain in Wales (a country full of mountains). But, to the serious walkers, climbers, and mountaineers it means a lot more. To them it's a place full of history, a place that gives them enormous pleasure, a place where they can find nature at its most unrefined, and a place in which they can find themselves.

I hope this book will enable us to appreciate this unique place, even more.

Robert Jones, 2007

Introduction

This book is about a single mountain: Snowdon, and it is necessary to differentiate 'Snowdon' from 'Snowdonia', the word which is now used to describe the area of north west Wales in which the mountain is a central peak. Throughout this book therefore, 'Snowdon' will refer to the mass that occupies most of the triangle between Llanberis, Penygwryd and Beddgelert. Likewise, 'Yr Wyddfa' will relate to the main summit of the massif.

For many thousands of years, this wild and rugged region of north Wales has been known to its inhabitants as Eryri, 'the abode of eagles'. However, Welsh scholars have more recently proposed a different interpretation and regard Eryri as 'the high land'. The earliest mention of the name in literature is found in a manuscript believed to have been written by the Welshman Nynniaw, or Nennius. In it we are told that King Gwrtheryn, also known to us as Vortigern, whilst seeking a safe retreat from the attacks of the English, came to the country called Gwynedd and found there in the mountains of Eryri a place which was fitted for his purpose and which he proceeded to fortify.

There seems to have been good reason for giving this name of Eryri to the Snowdonia area as eagles have inhabited its cliffs and cwms for as long as we know and have furnished bard and storyteller with many an image. Giraldus Cambrensis mentions the eagle of Snowdon, which perched every Thursday on a certain 'stone of destiny', in the hope that it could feed off the carcasses of men killed in battle. The place was evidently on the boundary between two cantrefs, where conflict often took place, though not with the weekly regularity that the bird expected – hence the saying that the eagle knows the place, but not the time, at which to find its prey. In the Elizabethan age, Thomas Price of Plas Iolyn sent a Snowdonian eagle on an errand to his brother poets, and his description of the "king of mountain fowl", dwelling on the "clear-cut heights above the rockbound tarn", makes it certain that he drew his description from actual sightings.

Fifty or so years later Thomas Johnson, the botanist, claimed the reason he failed in 1639 to get the rare plants he desired from the precipices of Carnedd Llywelyn, was that the small boy who was acting as his guide was "too much afraid of the eagles" to take him there. And in 1802, William Williams of Llandegai noted that "some wandering eagles are now and then in these times seen skulking in the precipices", but in the last hundred years or so, no further sightings have been recorded.

The English had their own name for this region, they called it Snowdon the mountain of snow. Camden, in his original edition of *Britannia* (1586), uses the expression *historicis Latinis Snaudonia*, though he was mistaken in supposing that the snow lay on the summits all year round because it was, and still is, a fairly common sight only during the winter months from October to April. Though in very cold years, remnants of drifts may even be found the north face of the Carneddau well into June. To add further confusion, 'Snowdon', as used by the older writers, invariably stood for the whole mountainous area which we now call 'Snowdonia', and never for the single summit to which the name is now restricted.

In the Anglo-Saxon *Chronicle*, one of the earliest instances of the use of the name says that in 1095 William Rufus came with his armies to 'Snawdun', and in 1188, Giraldus Cambrensis who was familiar with the Welsh Eryri, gives the English equivalent as 'Snaudune'. In 1230, Llywelyn the Great assumed the new title *Princeps Aberfraw Dominus Snawdon*, and it was obvious that he was not claiming dominion over a single peak, but as ruler of the whole region which in the *Mabinogion* is called the "strength of Gwynedd".

Snowdon is now accepted as the modern form of the Anglo-Saxon 'Snawdune', supposed to be a literal translation of Creigiau'r Eira, a mistaken rendering of Creigiau Eryri, the 'rocks of eagles'. Broadly speaking Eryri was composed of the two cantrefs of Arfon and Arllechwedd, and the two commotes of Nant Conwy and Eifionydd. Arfon and Arllechwedd together stretched over the central mass of mountains from Conwy to the Eifl (the Rivals); the dividing line between them being the river Cegin which flows into the sea at Port Penrhyn, while further south the border ran along the western bank of Nant Ffrancon, and over the Glyderau to Penygwryd. Eifionydd (which once formed a cantref with Ardudwy) was south of the main mass, and occupied the coastal plain between Abererch and Traeth Mawr, with Nant Conwy as another outlier, stretching from Trefriw to the source of the Conwy river. The chain of mountains around Ffestiniog, which although located in Ardudwy, were also included in the Snowdonia group.

Already it is apparent that this mountain possesses a wonderful 'mystical' aura and, indeed, many of the placenames of Snowdon have legends attached to them, and the better known of these are listed at the end of the book. Now, however, it is time to wander onto the mountain itself, but to appreciate the journey we must first try to understand how Snowdon was 'born'.

The Birth of Snowdon

Its geological structure and comparative geographic isolation give Snowdon a characteristic pyramid outline recognisable from distant viewpoints, from some of which it even appears symmetrical. In fact it is penetrated on all sides by cwms (hollows) with precipitous curving sides and, viewed from a neighbouring peak such as Moel Siabod, Snowdon today is obviously the remains of a mass from which much has been eroded. The steep cliffs surrounding the cwms and the sharp ridges which separate them provide physical attractions for the climber and striking views for the walker.

In *Fodinae Regales*, a book published in 1670, Sir John Pettus states that

> The usual method of historians is to begin with the Creation wherein I might tell you that when God breathed upon the face of the waters, that was a Petrefying Breath, and such Waters as were quiet and calm turned into Plains or Levelled Earth, and the Boisterous Waters into Hills and Mountains, according to the proportion of the Billows, and their Spaces into Vallies, which have ever since continued in those wonderful and pleasant Dimensions.

Such a conception may seem amusing now, but it offered an explanation for the origin of the scenery around Snowdon. In almost any upland region, the hills rising one above the other and alternating with one another, have the appearance of the undulating surface of a boisterous river or of waves breaking on a shelving shore. However, what Pettus could not be expected to have known, is that the hills and the valleys, as we see them, are not original features of the earth's surface unchanged since the beginning of time. Valleys have been carved out, not suddenly created; and the hills and mountains are the masses that nature's agents of erosion have not yet been able to wear away.

The first clue to the origin of Snowdon lies in the more or less angular masses of rock and screes that are so freely scattered on its slopes, and that originated in the steeper crags above. The mountains of today are built of the debris of the past, and they owe the character for which we admire them to the fact that they are disintegrating to provide materials for the mountains of future ages. This is a very slow process, and even over a generation, few are conscious of minute changes such as the distribution of individual stones, although anyone who has known a mountain long enough to become familiar with its features, can hardly fail to notice that change is taking place. A great rock may have fallen from a crag-face after a hard winter's frost; a river or stream in flood has cut its channel deeper; or a tarn or lake may have become perceptibly smaller. From a distance, the mountain seems unchanged, yet such incidents are part of that unremitting process of erosion to which every land surface is subjected.

The visitor will also be able to track of the rocks that protrude through the turf on the mountain, indicators of the stratification concealed by the soil. Sometimes these exposures run horizontally; sometimes they are steeply inclined; and sometimes they are curved; but in each case it is normally easy to envisage their continuation as strata beneath the turf. Where the slopes are too steep for soil to rest these strata are clearly visible, such as the great basin-like folds exposed on the face of Clogwyn Du'r Arddu.

The magnificence of rock-faces like Clogwyn Du'r Arddu (see image on page 117), and indeed Snowdon as a whole, is due to the rock that have been worn away. The action of rain and frost in disintegrating rocks, and of gravity, wind, and streams in removing the debris, turned what would probably have been a featureless high plateau with an undulating surface.

To the non-geologist, it may seem surprising that high mountains like Snowdon are the remains of trough-like folds, or that the summit should possess a basin-like (synclinal) structure. It would seem more appropriate for a mountain to have an arch-like (anticlinal) form, and a valley or other low ground to have a synclinal one. Yet when rocks are folded by high pressure, those at the crests of the folds tend to become stretched and crack easily, hence they are more easily weakened and worn away. The rocks in the troughs on the other hand, are squeezed together so become more

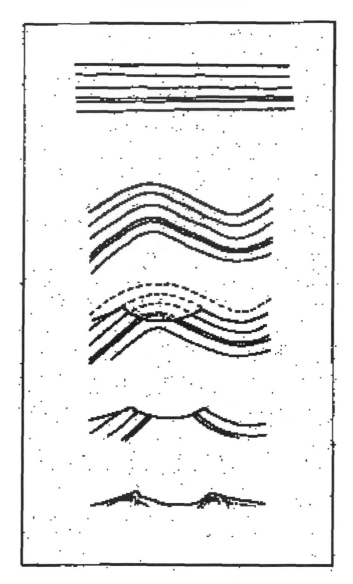

Fig. 1.Stages in the formation of mountains

compact and better able to resist erosion. Thus these harder rocks tend to remain as high ground after the rocks of the anticlines (arches) have been worn away (see Fig. 1, above).

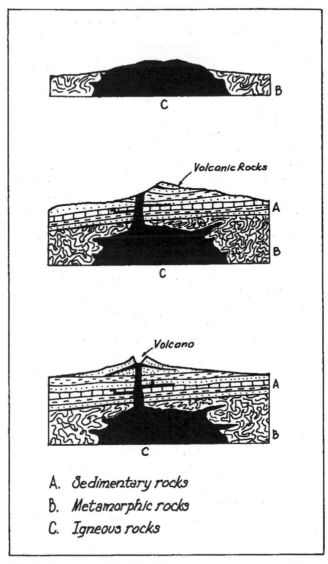

Fig. 2. Structure of the Earth's crust showing relationship between various rock types

The underlying rock structure of Snowdon is readily seen by walking up the Llanberis Path. The first exposed rocks are grey rust-weathering slates and sandstones; for about a quarter of a mile on either side of Halfway Station, there are darker slates, some blue-black. Beyond this, for a further half a mile or so, there are light-coloured, massive rocks of volcanic origin, often flinty in appearance. Still higher up, and for the last mile and a half, the route passes over more or less regularly arranged beds, of which some are speckled greenish-grey rocks composed of lava fragments, rough to the touch and deep brown on the weathered surfaces, while others are smooth and slaty. Towards the summit itself some of the beds contain the shells of marine animals, proof of the magnitude of the changes the land has undergone – the top of the highest mountain in England and Wales contains remains of life that was once on the sea floor!

The explanation of how these marine animals arrived on the summit lies millions of years in the past. Marine sediments accumulated in layers, together with debris such as lavas and ashes. Their present folded condition, to be seen in exposed rock-faces, is the result of lateral pressure due to movements in the earth's crust that squeezed the sediments, causing the layers to buckle and fold.

In a succession of strata resting one upon another, the lowest being the first to be laid down, every bed containing fossils (the remains of marine animals) is a deposit which must once have formed the floor of a sea, and each stratum is the record of a stage in the history of the earth, which tells us something about the conditions existing at the time it was formed.

Inspection of an exposed crag, or broken stone lying on the earth, shows a thin, superficial layer different in appearance from the material in the centre. This difference may be in colour, or softness, or porous attributes, but in each case the difference is due principally to exposure to the weather: the process known as weathering. Hence some of the volcanic rocks found on Snowdon are almost white, whilst the unweathered ones beneath the surface may be grey or nearly black.

Weathering usually takes place very slowly and involves mechanical disintegration as well as chemical alteration. Many minerals, the basic constituents of rocks, are decomposed by rainwater containing gases dissolved in it during its passage through the atmosphere, and some of them give rise to comparatively soft material that is easily washed away; when this is removed, the more resistant mineral particles, if any, are no longer held securely together, and they too are liable to be blown or washed away.

Some rocks are more resistant and the results of weathering vary according to the chemical composition of the constituent minerals, but the process eventually results in the tiny loose particles that are the essential ingredients of clay or of sand. Eventually this material is carried away in streams and comes to rest on the floor of the sea into which the stream or river flows. It accumulates together with the material produced by the destructive action of the waves upon the rocks of the coasts.

During its transportation by streams and rivers, the material is graded naturally and sorted according to the size of particle, with smaller particles being carried further than larger, heavier ones. Hence pebbles are found on the shore nearest land, whilst the smaller particles are found as sand near the sea, and the even smaller particles (the essential ingredients of clay) under the sea. In addition to the land-derived sediments, the shells or other calcareous hard parts of marine animals also accumulate which produce the deposits that will eventually become limestone.

As the seas recede over thousands of years, the sea-bed deposits of one geological age have become the dry-land rocks of the next. Sediments that originated as mud gave rise to rocks such as shale; deposits of sand became sandstones; accumulations of pebbles gave rise to conglomerates; whilst the shells or bones of animals, or the remains of plants that became embedded in the sediments were fossilised. So sedimentary rocks tell us something of the past geography of the region in which they occur .

The other main type of rock – igneous – is formed by volcanic eruption. Such activity often results in vast quantities of ash and fine dust.The other product from a volcano is lava, rock which flows in a molten state, spreading around the area close to its emergence. After a volcanic eruption, both ash and lava settle on the sedimentary rocks (Fig. 2).

Because they occur as beds that were laid down one upon another, sedimentary rocks are classified in the order in which they were formed and the relative age of a lava can be determined by position in the associated sediments because it must be newer

ERA	PERIODS (ROCK SYSTEMS)	million years	SNOWDONIA PRINCIPAL GEOLOGICAL EVENTS	
CAINOZOIC (QUATERNARY)	HOLOCENE	RECENT 0·01	Finishing touches to surface features- and drainage. Ice Age or Glacial Period.	WITH PARTIAL ENCROACHMENT OF SEA AT RARE INTERVALS
	PLEISTOCENE			
CAINOZOIC (TERTIARY)	PLIOCENE	2	Denudation and general shaping of present mountains.	
	MIOCENE	7		LAND CONDITIONS
	OLIGOCENE	26	MOUNTAIN BUILDING (Slight effects) 'Alpine Storm.'	
	EOCENE	38		
	PALÆOCENE	54		
MESOZOIC	CRETACEOUS	65	Probable submergence beneath 'Chalk Sea' and production of comparatively even surface.	
	JURASSIC	136	Long-continued denudation probably with partial return of sea during Jurassic Period.	
	TRIASSIC	195		
PALAEOZOIC	PERMIAN	225	Desert conditions, arid climate.	
		280	MOUNTAIN BUILDING (Slight effects) 'Hercynian Movements'	
	CARBONIFEROUS		Lowering of level with perhaps encroachments of sea over margins of Snowdonia.	
	DEVONIAN	345	Widespread uplift; rocks thrown into folds; shales converted into slates.	MARINE CONDITIONS
	SILURIAN	395	MOUNTAIN BUILDING 'Caledonian Movements', profound effects.	
	ORDOVICIAN	440	Intense VOLCANIC ACTIVITY Deposition of sediments that became the Slates of Blaenau Ffestiniog.	
		500		
	CAMBRIAN		Deposition of sediments that became the Slates of Bethesda, Llanberis & Nantlle.	
EOZOIC	PRE-CAMBRIAN	570	Land conditions with volcanoes ending long period of denudation and earth movements: details unknown.	LAND CONDITIONS AT END OF ERA
			MOUNTAIN BUILDING	
	ORIGIN OF EARTH ▶	4500		

ROCK SYSTEMS STILL REPRESENTED AMONGST THE MOUNTAINS OF SNOWDONIA.

Fig. 3. Geological history of Snowdonia

than those upon which it rests, yet older than those which have been laid down upon it. By studying the successive layers of sedimentary rocks and the fossils by which each is characterised, it is

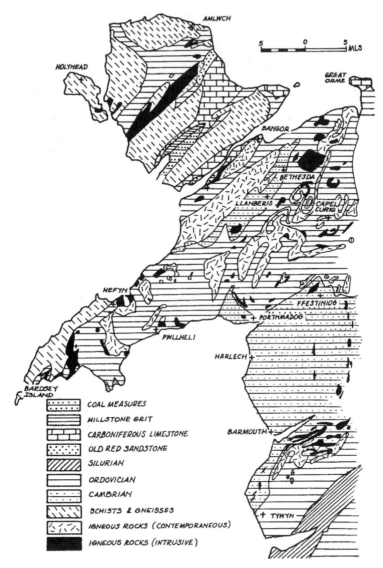

Fig. 4. The soild geology of Gwynedd

therefore possible to determine the order in which the strata were formed, even if the strata have become folded, eroded, or only partially exposed. The main classification of strata are shown in Figure 3.

To fully appreciate the geological features of Snowdon it is necessary to also look at those of the area around the massif. As previously discussed, an essential feature of Snowdonia's geology is that its rocks are all very old, in fact by looking at the geological map of North Wales (Fig. 4), it can be seen that Anglesey has some of the world's oldest rocks – from the Pre-Cambrian era. These rocks are almost without fossils, being formed in a world where life had only just begun.

These same primordial rocks continue under the Menai Strait then meet the rocks of the next era – the Cambrian – that rise high to form Moel Eilio, Carnedd y Filiast and Elidir Fawr. These merge into the rocks from which Snowdon itself was formed – the Ordovician – and this band also includes the Glyderau, Carneddau and practically all the rest of the National Park.

Snowdonia's geology has not only provided some of the best examples of these various eras, it also gave rise to the actual names that are now associated with these eras, hence the names Cambrian, Ordovician and Silurian which were invented by the pioneer geologists. 'Cambrian' comes from Cambria, the name that was revived to describe Wales by early Romantic writers; 'Ordovician' commemorates the Ordovices, a tribe living in north Wales before and during the Roman period; and 'Silurian' is named after the Silures, a tribe that inhabited South Wales.

The historical geology of Snowdon (Fig. 5) shows how, at the start of the Cambrian period, 600 million years ago, what is now Snowdonia was merely a patch on the floor of an ocean, and remained so during the next 100 million years while a great depth of Cambrian rocks was deposited, the material of which came from the decay of the pre-Cambrian mountains that undoubtedly surrounded this ocean. This laying down of ocean-bed rocks continued through a further 100 million years of Ordovician and Silurian times until the trough (or geosyncline) in which the ocean lay 'sagged' ever deeper into the earth's crust due to the weight of more and more rocks being laid down.

As the Silurian period was succeeded by the Devonian, the ocean was at last pushed aside and land, including what is now Snowdonia, began to appear above the water, forced up by immense pressures operating through the earth's crust. As this

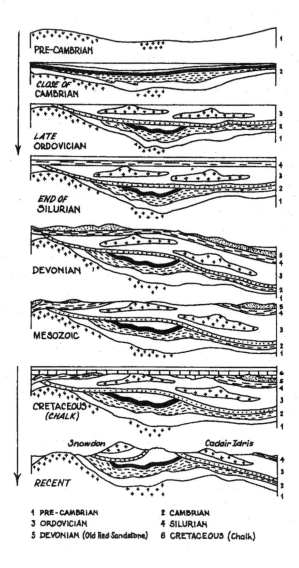

Fig. 5. The Emergence of Snowdon

new land appeared it was immediately exposed to the forces of erosion. The Silurian rocks, being on top of the pile were the first to be eroded and in time were swept away almost entirely. Then the Ordovician strata eroded, but even though this erosion was quite considerable over most of the area, parts of it remain almost as stumps, which are the basis of the mountains we see today.

Of the four ancient geological periods that were instrumental in the development of Snowdonia, it is the Ordovician that is the most important, not just because its rocks occupy so much of the surface today but because it was a time of great volcanic activity. Whilst the sedimentary rocks were being laid down, volcanoes were erupting on the ocean floor, producing enormous quantities of lavas and ashes. There then followed long periods of inactivity during which further sediments covered the volcanic rocks until the eruptions started again, with some of the volcanoes emerging as huge islands in the Ordovician sea.

The alternating settling periods and volcanic outbursts resulted in a complex layering of sedimentary and volcanic rocks. It was further complicated by the cooling together of the material that poured out of the volcanoes, together with the large amounts of molten and gaseous material which never erupted but remained amongst the sedimentary layers, both formed the granites, felsites and dolerites which as they themselves have now eroded, form much of the land today. Repeated phases of earth movement, which rose to a crescendo soon after the Silurian period, threw the whole strata of these sedimentary and igneous rocks into a series of upfolds, downfolds and fractures which are now part of the scenery that we see today.

The Ordovician volcanoes were widespread, their distribution today being marked by the peaks of hard igneous rocks which still stand high while the softer rocks around them have long since been dissolved and washed away by the nearby rivers. Although we know about the existence of Snowdonia's ancient volcanoes, it is difficult to locate precisely where they erupted because their craters and cones have also eroded. What is now left are the last remains of the lava fields and the exploded matter (pyroclatic rocks), so even though it might sometimes look like one, Snowdon itself was not a volcano similar to, say, Mount Etna.

The Devonian period which succeeded the Silurian was the age of Caledonian mountain building, so called because it produced that series of parallel hills and valleys aligned north-east to south-west which is still evident in Scotland (Caledonia). In fact this geosyncline stretched all the way from Wales through Scotland to Scandinavia. The pressure needed to cause this folding of the earth's crust is thought to have been produced from the south-east, the rocks of Snowdonia then becoming crumpled against the immovable block or pre-Cambrian rocks in the region of Anglesey.

By the time this long process of distortion subsided the block of rocks from which the Snowdon massif was to be formed lay in the centre of the strata. Such rocks, bent downwards into a trough (syncline) are more likely to be further hardened by compression which is probably the reason Snowdon has not been eroded to the extent of some of its neighbouring mountain summits. In fact, these down-curving rock beds can be best seen on the east face after a light snow fall, when they are highlighted by the weather.

The detailed structure of Snowdonia is highly complex and the first impression can be that the steeply tilted rock strata seem to slope in a variety of ways, in no particular order. Yet a simple basic pattern can be established, consisting of a trough in the north and a broad wave in the south, lying alongside each other on a north-east to south-west alignment. The bottom of the trough runs through Moel Hebog, Snowdon, the Glyderau and the Carneddau, whilst the top of the wave is midway between Moelwyn Mawr and Cader Idris. This whole wave, or arch, formation is known as the Harlech Dome, as it is centred on the Rhinog range of mountains near Harlech.

The visual evidence of the trough can be clearly seen looking up Nant Ffrancon from Bethesda to Ogwen on the A5. Across the valley on the flank of the Glyder range the strata are sloping towards the south. They then form the north side of the syncline which then curves round underground and reappears sloping upwards towards the south on Tryfan. Beyond Tryfan the beds arch over again and once more dip towards the south on Gallt-yr-Ogof. This is only a minor ripple, and to see the rocks really climbing up the north side of the Harlech Dome, view Cnicht or the Moelwyn range, where the strata rise boldly towards the south in many of the rocks at the northern end of the Rhinog range.

So, such is the geological diversity of Snowdonia that each

summit stands apart not merely by external appearances but also by its original composition and structure, and Snowdon is a typical sandwich of sedimentary and volcanic materials.

One of the most important geological aspects of Snowdon is the range of metals that exist in the rock formations. The effect their existence has had on the industrial history of the mountain is discussed later in the book, but in geological terms it is important to acknowledge the wide range of these substances that can be found. The major ones are copper, lead, zinc, silver, gold, iron, and manganese, the ores of which are also the result of igneous activity. Their presence is frequently associated with fault lines, having been forced in hot liquid or gaseous form into cracks in the surrounding rocks where they have subsequently cooled and solidified to form the metallic veins, or lodes.

Another important geological aspect of Snowdon results from the other major class of rocks found on the massif – metamorphic. These may have originated as igneous or sedimentary types but have then been converted by heat or pressure. One type of rock produced this way is very important to Snowdonia – slate. These were originally shales deposited in Cambrian times which, during the Silurian and Devonian times underwent immense lateral pressure which moved the rocks into waves which eventually were compressed and hardened into slate.

Since the end of the Silurian period, there are no further clues to what happened to the basic underlying rocks in the area. Some geologists think that Snowdonia has remained above sea level ever since the Silurian days, and that no further rocks have been deposited. However, others believe that after the Silurian period, Snowdonia was submerged probably more than once, and that later rocks such as Triassic or the Cretaceous were laid down but after again being raised above the sea, were totally removed by further erosion.

Whatever actually happened to the basic rocks, probably the most important period to have an effect on the landscape we actually see today was the Pleistocene period, which roughly corresponds to the Great Ice Age, the glaciers of which disappeared a mere ten thousand years ago. As these immense masses of ice made their slow way down from the mountains, they

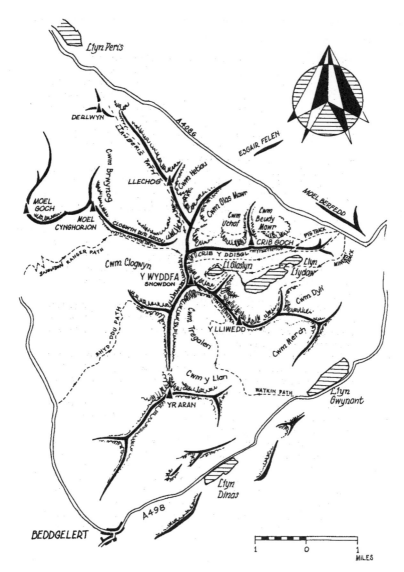

Fig. 6. The Ridges of Snowdonia

smoothed valleys such as Nant Ffrancon, into their current U-shaped forms. Many of the corrie cliffs, knife-edged ridges, and screes are also the result of glacial action, as are the deep moraine-edged lakes. In fact, practically every geological aspect which now forms the features of Snowdon, is the product of the Ice Age.

The Snowdon massif today takes the form of a star-shaped pattern of six ridges radiating from Yr Wyddfa, which enclose deep rock basins with steep rock walls. The two shortest ridges divide from Bwlch Main to the southwest, enclosing Cwm Clogwyn and Cwm Llan. Two more, of intermediate length, are the Crib Coch ridge which runs out to Pen-y-pass and the Lliwedd ridge that runs to Gallt-y-Wenallt, both of which are named after their respective satellite summits. These two are the highest ridges on Snowdon, and between them they encircle Cwm Glaslyn, Cwm Llydaw and Cwm Dyli in the vast amphitheatre of the 'Snowdon Horseshoe'. A northern ridge runs to Llanberis flanking the Llanberis Pass and finally, the longest ridge runs out beyond Moel Eilio to the northwest (see Fig. 6).

To understand the extent to which glaciers created this modern outline of Snowdon, it is necessary to relate their action to its form prior to the Ice Age. In some ways this is problematic since the more rock the ice removed, the less pre-glacial landscape remains. However there is some evidence to help such a reconstruction. For example, the most striking feature of Snowdon's landscape is the contrast between relatively gentle, rounded summit slopes and sheer rock walls excavated often hundreds of metres deep into them. Then there is the large number of troughs separating Snowdon from its neighbours. Also, in some places satellite summits not much lower than Yr Wyddfa lie closer still, and the mountain flanks are particularly precipitous in Nant Gwynant and the Llanberis Pass.

Although it is this dramatic discordance between rounded summits and rock walls that marks the interface between the Ice Age and pre-glacial relief, the remnant of the pre-glacial summit is restricted to the west side of the mountain, in the rounded slopes west of Yr Wyddfa, Carnedd Ugain, Bwlch Main and Gyrn Las, and with smaller areas on the lower spurs of Cwm Clogwyn, the Llanberis Pass plus the southwest crests of Moel Cynghorion and Moel Eilio. The eastern slopes on the other hand have been largely destroyed through the action of a series of cirque glaciers. Hence as was said at the beginning of this chapter, Snowdon has its asymmetrical profile.

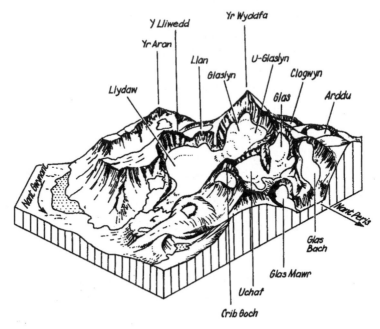

Fig. 7. The Snowdon Glaciers

To appreciate how glaciers developed the landscape that now exists, we need only study the typical weather conditions that exist on the massif today. Owing to the mean winter temperatures of minus 5°C on Yr Wyddfa and an annual precipitation of approx 200 inches at the summit and about 120 inches generally over the rest of the mountain, snow tends to lie continuously in the sheltered gullies for over four months of the year, and intermittently on the rest of the massif for about six months.

Imagine now the much lower temperatures during the Ice Age, and it is most likely these would have lowered the snowline, or firnline, so that the whole of the mountain would have been permanently covered with snow. Much of the snow would also no doubt have been susceptible to drifting and avalanching, most of which would have taken place in the gullies. The snows would have alternately thawed and re-frozen over many years, which in turn would have weathered the underlying rock to produce the debris which would eventually be carried in the glaciers.

Consequently, although ice is weaker than rock, the glaciers were very powerful erosive agents, the debris of rock fragments held in the glacial ice acting like sandpaper to abrade the softer rock underneath. After the initial abrasion, gravity would have worked to move the deposits down the mountain, where they eventually came to rest forming a moraine, having in the meantime gouged out the initial gully into a much wider cirque or 'amphitheatre', which in Wales is more commonly known as a 'cwm'. On the Snowdon massif, there is much evidence to testify to these processes having taken place, as can be seen by looking at the main cwms themselves (Fig. 7).

The four small northern cirques of Cwm Glas, Cwm Glas Mawr, Cwm Glas Bach and Cwm Uchaf are partially concealed by both the awe-inspiring cliffs flanking the Llanberis Pass and culminating in the peaks of Llechog, Gyrn Las, Carnedd Ugain and Crib Goch, and also the two large buttresses of Clogwyn Mawr and Dinas Mot which hang over the valley. In fact being positioned as they are, and having had a restricted development, they are typical of the main cirques found on the massif.

The central cirques of Cwm Llan, Cwm Clogwyn and Cwm Du'r Arddu are larger and more mature forms with compound basins that are believed to have been occupied by ice more than once. All possess large moraines and the cirques of Clogwyn and Du'r Arddu contain enclosed rock – and moraine-dammed lakes, whereas Cwm Llan is an amalgamation of up to three cirques. In Cwm Llan the highest rock wall is directly below Snowdon's summit and faces south and is believed to be older than the steep cliffs that have been cut into the west wall facing Cwm Tregalan. Erosion by the Tregalan and Clogwyn glaciers together acted to form the arete (serrated, knife-edged ridge) at Bwlch Main.

Like Cwm Llan, Cwm Clogwyn is symmetrical but with an east wall higher than the west, due in part to the greater available relief in the east, and the locally reinforcing effect of the intrusive rhyolite. A step extends across the cirque exit higher than the surrounding area, and this impounds three small lakes. The Clogwyn glacier also left a trail of moraines beyond the cirque, one of which impounds Llyn Ffynnon-y-gwas.

Cwm Du'r Arddu has a more irregular plan with a small rock wall in the east leading to an almost vertical west wall with a superb exposure of the folded rock strata. This rock wall was continually undercut by a small but powerful cirque glacier, and large slabs and wedges of rock now litter the moraines beyond the rock-basin lake. As previously mentioned, the Snowdon Horseshoe is a prime example of cirque glaciation, with each of four rock basins superimposed on its neighbour, forming a descending 'cirque staircase' almost 5km in length. This staircase commences high on the west wall of Cwm Glaslyn with the smallest rock basin – Upper Glaslyn – and then proceeds down through the successively larger basins of Cwm Glaslyn, Cwm Llydaw and Cwm Dyli.

Both Glaslyn and Llydaw basins contain large rock-dammed lakes, and are separated by rock thresholds. It is thought that the Glaslyn glacier was established first, and this then proceeded down Cwm Llydaw where it excavated the basin that now contains Llyn Llydaw and at the same time left the *roches moutonées* and striated surfaces that can now be observed below the steep rock walls of Y Lliwedd. In fact, the Pig Track follows a broad ridge on the side of Cwm Llydaw in line with the Glaslyn rock barrier, and is probably a remnant of the valley floor eroded by the Glaslyn and Llydaw glaciers, and it is this joint Glaslyn-Llydaw ice flow that eventually excavated the Dyli basin, and abraded the two huge *roches moutonées* of Craig Aderyn and Clogwyn Pen Llechen.

Living off Snowdon

One cold, wet, day, as I was returning down the Llanberis Path, I met a farmer herding his sheep. Seeing this solitary man and his dog made me realise that to the tourists and travellers, Snowdon was and still is, a place for adventure, excitement, and leisure. To the indigenous people who had, and still have, to make a living off the mountain, it was not so adventurous, exciting, or leisurely. Until man can harness natural forces and develop machinery to control his environment, his choice of habitation is dominated by the physical features of the land he occupies. That choice is limited by such factors as topography, climate and prevailing winds, soil-types with their differing covers such as forest,moorland or marsh and, of course, water supplies.

At the start of the Neolithic period the windswept coastlands and cliffs of Gwynedd were probably fairly open ground, but the immediate hinterland and the hills rising from it were clad with an unbroken forest cover, probably to a height of some 1,500 feet in the inland valleys, though the prevailing westerly winds would have possibly restricted tree growth to a lower level on the seaward slopes. Sessile oak predominated, but alder was also found on the wetter parts, and even birch on the upper forest fringes. Furthermore the areas sufficiently open to settlement would have been limited to those people who knew how to use stone axes or antler picks. The area around Snowdon therefore offered no ready supplies of such tools to Palaeolithic man, and it wasn't until the art of polishing stone tools began in the Neolithic age that the igneous rock outcrops could be utilised.

The Neolithic phase, which probably lasted a mere five hundred years or so in Wales, was a time of revolutionary change in both customs and manners. It was a period of intense intellectual vigour and activity, as people learned to master the domestic arts of grain-growing, stock-rearing and pottery-making, and to build for themselves fixed dwellings rather than the nomadic ones of their predecessors. But it was the physical imprint that is still stamped indelibly even on the modern day dwellers of north Wales, that these dark, sturdy people were responsible for, and remembered by.

Around 2,000 B.C. Snowdon was invaded next by the Beaker people who penetrated the area probably by an overland route across the Shropshire hills. They were so called from the distinctive vessels normally buried with their dead, and of which many remains have been found in the area. They were a dominant people, largely pastoralists and hunters, and not inclined to farming. They subdued the earlier Neolithic population, took over their grazing grounds, and assumed the role of leadership in the communities. During the next few centuries, the Beaker and Neolithic populations of the highland zones of north Wales settled down with each other, and their customs and traditions merged to their mutual benefit. In fact, the Early and Middle Bronze Ages were a time of comparative quiet, and it was more the effect of the weather that influenced the next major change. The dry, boreal period which prevailed during the greater part of the Bronze Age greatly denuded Snowdon's forest growth, and made possible for the first time, the penetration and settlement of its flanks and surrounding valleys.

The latter years of the Bronze Age and the early centuries of the Iron Age brought the next period of upheaval and shifting of peoples, mainly due to the further climatic changes, and the use of available land. The wet, stormy weather of this period drove the inhabitants of Snowdon back to the higher reaches away from the woods and luscious undergrowth that had started to spring up and choke the valleys. The huts of these Iron Age people were normally sited in circles on a sheltered ledge having a south or south-west aspect, and on dry soils that could not become boggy with rain. Adjoining them were usually small paddocks, divided by low walls of loose stones, and varying in size from a few hundred square yards to three or four acres, the larger fields being cultivated. A group of these hut circles definitely existed near the spot where the outflow of Llyn Llydaw enters Cwm Dyli, as the remains of flint arrow-heads, stone implements, and also slag refuse from the smelting of copper ore have been excavated from the site.

Although the centuries of the early Iron Age which immediately precede the Roman occupation of Snowdonia are somewhat obscure, it is known that somewhere between 500 B.C. and 300 B.C. Celtic traders and settlers were pushing into the hill districts on the outskirts of Snowdon, especially the Ordovices who brought with them the Celtic language from which modern Welsh is derived. These new inhabitants also brought with them the rites and teachings known as Druidism which became the general religion of the tribes of north Wales. They also were what could be considered as the first teachers, giving oral instruction in a range of subjects as diverse as philosophy, astronomy, and even medical lore. Unfortunately , because their teaching was mainly oral, very little written proof of their skills or knowledge remains, which in turn leaves the mind open to conjecture regarding some of their rituals and rites.

It was into an almost 'mystical' land that the Romans entered, but it was also a turbulent one which they had to conquer in order to survive. This they finally did by their campaigns of A.D. 75-80, and in fact, in the third and fourth centuries, even enlisted the help of the hill-dwellers to defend the area from marauders from Ireland who were continually harrying them. Although no Roman forts have been found on Snowdon itself, their presence is amply recorded in such places as Caernarfon (Segontium), Chester (Deva), and Caer Llugwy between Capel Curig and Betws-y-coed. Although the Romans might have been remembered for the rule they brought to the somewhat barbaric tribes of Snowdonia, they will probably best be acknowledged for the way in which they helped by clearing the uplands around Snowdon for both settlement and cultivation. It was therefore a fertile land that the Irish tribes finally invaded after the withdrawal of the Roman troops. There is little material evidence of their presence apart from a few memorial stones bearing Ogham inscriptions, and the name commonly given to their clusters of hut-circles locally is 'cytiau'r Gwyddelod' (the Irishmen's huts).

Irish-speaking tribes certainly inhabited the Snowdon area in the fifth century, and there was much fighting with the local Welsh people. There are stories told of an Irish city at Muria'r Dre (town walls) near Cwm Dyli, and a battle in which the Welsh were defeated at Bwlch y Gwyddyl (the Irishmen's Pass) near Penygwryd. About the year 400, Cunedda and his 'sons' (actually his tribesmen) arrived from the Scottish border to assist the Welsh overthrow the Irish tribes, and in fact subsequently founded the locally ruling dynasty from which later kings were to trace their descent. Furthermore, the names of the old counties of north and mid-Wales are believed to have been derived from the names of these 'children' among whom the land was partitioned. With this new era we also enter a time of mystery and legends, the most famous being those linked to Arthur.

Arthur was probably the great general Aurelius Ambrosius and acted as the representative of what was left of the imperial traditions. He would possibly have held the office of *Dux Bellorum,* and had a mobile army at his disposal to move swiftly to any point where action was required. His role therefore was to revive some of the Roman order and discipline against the growing lawlessness in the wake of the retreat of the Romans, and also to maintain a constant battle against the Saxon invaders.

Life in the hill-forts continued well into the Dark Ages, and they were possibly re-occupied later, from time to time, when invasion threatened. But in the sixth and seventh centuries the inhabitants were moving away from these shelters, and even occupying the ruins of their local Roman strongholds. Others would venture on to a shoulder of the hill below a fortress, or at the head of a nearby valley. A feature peculiar to many of the Dark Age and early medieval dwelling sites in Snowdonia was the presence of a rectangular earthen platform, dug out of the hillside, on which the dwellings were erected, nestling into the shelter of the slope. There were usually two buildings, a house and a cattle shed, facing onto a yard enclosed by a low bank. These steadings were usually situated on the open moorland, between 600 and 1,300 feet.

The walls of the houses were made of earth mixed with stones, or of wattle hurdles fixed to small upright poles which were sunk into an earthen sill. The ridge pole of the roof was supported by two or three curved principals, or forks, rising from the floor near the centre of the room. The roof was a thatch of heather or rushes, or a covering of turf, supported on rods which ran from the ridge pole to the posts of the side walls. The floor was of beaten earth or pebbles and the hearth was a single stone slab, generally occupying a central position towards the back of the house with a hole in the roof let the smoke escape.

Such primitive dwellings could be quickly raised by unskilled labour, when required, which greatly aided the mobility of the owners when under threat . In fact, the favourite manoeuvre was for them to transfer themselves and their cattle to the fastness of Snowdon. Crops were ploughed in before they abandoned their old homes, and then new, temporary houses would be built in the shelter of Snowdon's slopes. Fortunately for these folk, the heavily armoured Saxon or Norman soldiers could not, or usually dared not, follow. The winds and rain of Snowdon were powerful allies of the Welsh; more than one army, starting out in great numbers, found itself soaked, floundering in quagmires, and forced to retreat.

It was the laws of Hywel Dda that gave Wales its first systematic partitioning of ownership. By the tenth century, each of the small kingdoms of Wales was partitioned into a number of districts called *cantrefi* (literally a hundred townships), each of which was itself sub-divided into two or more *cymydau* or 'commotes'. It is thought that a cantref may have represented the original land of a single tribe, whereas the commote and the *tref* (township) was the smaller and more effective unit of administration of the Middle Ages.

Each *tref* was not a cluster of houses as the name might imply in modern times, instead it was simply a division of the countryside in the commote, over which the farms straggled. Every homestead in the *tref* had attached to it a few acres of arable and meadow land. The holding, together with the house, barn, and outbuildings was then termed a *tyddyn.* As the basis of Welsh society was tribal, the lands of the *trefi* were generally occupied and worked on by large family groups, each claiming descent from a common ancestor. The actual land of each individual family was called a *gwely* (literally: a bed) and the small-holding was then known as the gwely of the person who first occupied it. On the death of the founder of the *gwely*, the inheritance was divided amongst his sons in equal portions. Such division of land incurred under the Welsh system of inheritance is one factor which, in the course of time, has lead to the small and irregular-shaped scattered holdings and lonely farms which are such a characteristic of the landscape on Snowdon.

Time and time again in the history of Wales, Snowdon has proved the final retreat of earlier settlers, especially as a stronghold to repel the invaders from the north east. For this reason, the traditions of these civilisations have tended to be preserved in these hills. At present, the Snowdon hills preserve some of the last remnants of the indigenous peasant cultures of Wales, and a language far older than the English tongue. Furthermore, even though the Romans, Irish, or Anglo-Saxons may have had an enriching influence on them, their traditions and customs are definitely their own.

Since medieval times, both the land on Snowdon itself and its immediate surroundings has been owned by private estates. The earliest mention of such landowning is to be found in the charter granted in 1198 by Llywelyn ap Iorwerth to the Cistercian Abbey of Aberconwy. Amongst other gifts to the abbey were the lands of Nanhwynen (Nant Gwynant) the boundary of which was clearly stated: "On the north-west side the boundary ran from Aber Colwyn, in the village of Beddgelert, along the Colwyn stream to its source at Bwlch Cwm Llein [Cwm Llan], thence along the edge of the rocks to the head of Wyddfa Fawr, thence to Grib Goch and by 'Wregyssauc' to the Seat of Peris [Pen-y-pass]".

Though it is now part of a National Park and a Nature Reserve in its own right, one can still trace the most recent owners of the land. The south east of the mountain, including Cwm Dyli, is part of the Baron Hill Estate, owned by the William Bulkeley family. Most of the north and west of the mountain was part of the Faenol Estate, owned by the Assheston Smith family. The remaining, south western area was owned by a number of smaller estates (see Fig 8, below).

The estates were rented out on an annual basis but it was only the actual land that was officially rented – all other items such as game, the animal stock, timber, mining rights, were retained by the estate owners. As already mentioned, the land around the base and also on the slopes of Snowdon was initially covered by forest, but because the tenant farmers' main source of livelihood was farming, deforestation became widespread to convert the land to pasture. In turn, the pasture higher up on the slopes became less useful for grazing cattle, so instead, the farmers allowed their sheep to fully roam these higher parts, keeping their cattle on the lower areas.

In the early seventeenth century, a typical farmer would grow a small acreage of oats in a valley such as Gwynant, have a couple of cows near his cottage the lower slopes, and then let his sheep or goats roam on the lower slopes in winter, and on the higher ones in the summer. The main drawback however, was that these basic farms were too small to be profitable, and in any case, the tenant farmers had no incentive to over-produce; hence they remained 'ticking-over', producing just enough produce to enable themselves to pay the rent and buy or barter basic food supplies. Until the 1960s, walkers could often encounter cattle grazing near the zig-zags on the Snowdon Ranger, and also near Half-Way House on the Llanberis Path. Unfortunately, grazing animals tend to devour the best grasses and now there remains very little good cattle-grazing pasture on Snowdon. This harsh grassland is now the domain of the mountain sheep, and these animals have figured prominently in the economy of Snowdon and the surrounding area.

Until fairly recent times the rural communities of Snowdon were largely self-sufficient, and only on rare occasions did the countryman find it necessary to venture outside his community or locale to search for the means of life. Most inhabitants of such rural communities were born, lived and died within the narrow confines of their own localities, and most realised their ambitions within their own communities, to which they were so often bound by ties of blood, family, and neighbourliness. But the rural neigh-bourhood was something more than a social entity – it was an economic one too.

All the food required by the community could be produced locally. They had animals that could supply milk, meat, skins, and wool. There were fields, gardens and sometimes orchards that supplied cereals, root crops, fruit and vegetables. In most parts of Snowdonia, until the end of the nineteenth century, farming depended almost entirely on a wide range of hand tools, a large

Fig. 8. Land Ownership of Snowdon

labour force and the co-operative effort of relatives and neighbours during the busy periods of the farming year. This mutual
assistance in farm work was central to the success of the community as a whole. On the one hand there was co-operation and the
co-ownership of implements such as a seed drill or mowing
machine between a number of farmers. On the other hand there
was co-operation between true farmers and a large number of
non-farming cottagers and smallholders, many of whom
possessed less than five acres of land.

The tools and implements of agriculture were few and simple, and farming was a manual art rather than the series of mechanical processes that it is today. Furthermore, no farm could exist as an independent and separate unit as most modern ones can. For example, few farms of less than eighty acres kept a bull, yet the income of all medium sized farms, especially in north Wales depended very largely on the sale of store cattle and butter.

The bull was an essential farm animal, especially the Welsh Blacks, but as only one farm in five possessed a bull, there was a constant traffic of cows from one farm to another throughout the summer months, to maintain an economic equilibrium in the area as a whole. No cash was exchanged for the service of these bulls; instead the debt was paid for by providing labour in the hay harvest, or some other busy occasion. Likewise, only one farm in eight kept a boar, but bacon pigs were also an important store animal, so a similar movement of these animals also took place on a regular basis. As with the sharing of animal services, the farmers shared their labour force too, to keep their individual overheads to a minimum. Therefore on certain occasions such as sheep shearing and potato picking, the labour force grew enormously.

The co-operative nature of the society around Snowdon was perhaps most clearly seen in the hayfields, for not only did neighbouring farmers help one another in harvesting this vital crop, but their wives and serving maids, together with local cottagers and their families, all joined forces to help. This help was especially useful in very wet years to enable the hay to be harvested speedily. The corn harvests however, were a matter for the individual farmers and there was little co-operation required as cereal crops were grown for self-consumption. Wheat was used in the home, oats for feeding the horses, and barley for feeding the cattle and pigs. The major drawback of cereal crops though was the time taken to sow and reap them.

Corn was usually sown broadcast from a basket or linen sheet; it was weeded with a forked stick or weeding hook, and harvested with a scythe. In normal years it would have taken an experienced scyther at least a full day to cut an acre of corn, and another half-day to bind it into sheaves. In very wet years however, when the rain and wind (which all regular walkers on Snowdon have no doubt experienced) had flattened the crop, it would have to be harvested with a sickle instead, making it an extremely slow and often dangerous task. The farmers were often forced to look elsewhere for extra labour at harvest-time, and instead of depending on farming neighbours, who were often themselves fully occupied, they used non-farming cottagers from the local vicinity such as Llanberis or Beddgelert. Quite often, the cottagers were largely dependent on their local farmers for a means of living. Whilst the farmers only paid each other with an exchange of labour, the cottagers were paid in kind. They were given a pat of butter, a jug of milk, a little cheese, a sack of swedes, or a sack of corn.

Alternatively, a day's labour in the hayfield might have been reimbursed by the farmer carting a load of coal from Caernarfon, or a cartful of manure for the cottagers' gardens. The cottagers were also allowed to plant potatoes in a neighbouring farmer's fields. The cottager supplied the seed potatoes, and the farmer prepared, weeded and fertilised the crop. In return, the cottager then undertook to work a fixed number of days linked to the number of rows of potatoes being grown.

In order to have large cattle stocks, the main problem facing Snowdon farmers was the production of sufficient hay to last through the winter months. There was insufficient lowland to cultivate for hay, and although many farmers tried to cultivate hay on the higher slopes, the inclement weather prevented success. In the late nineteenth and early twentieth centuries, a gradual change in farming methods took place, and by the mid 1930s the largely self-sufficient economy gave way to a more specialised dairying one. This change of emphasis completely altered the pattern of work on most Welsh farms, bringing about the decline of the farm servant, and a change in the livelihood of cottagers.

As a result of such limited opportunities, some tenant farmers took up schemes to raise supplementary income. One such activity was mining, which enabled them to earn money to buy the food and clothes they could not normally afford. This mining was done either as individuals, or as part-time labour for the various mine owners. Farmers also used the uplands as a source of non-monetary income, in that they harvested peat to heat their dwellings in the bitterly cold, winter months without having to pay for coal, which was not only itself expensive, but in some instances, could not be physically transported to the remoter parts of the mountain. If you look carefully when walking on Snowdon, you can still see the ruins of some of the drying houses that the farmers built near the peat bogs, especially on the southern slopes.

As if the Welsh hill farmer didn't face enough problems earning an inadequate income, actual living conditions were often poor too. The traditional houses of rural Wales owe their design and layout to a complex interaction of geological, geographical, economic and social factors. The nature of the climate, and the availability of suitable building materials had their effect on determining the type of house found in a particular area. The major part of Gwynedd is stone country so this was an area of dry-stone walls, and slate tile roofs. There were dwellings whose walls consisted of huge boulders, and there were others where narrow slabs of slate from Llanberis were used for wall construction. Most of the cottages were small with walls of great thickness and all windows were at the front of the house. Chimney places were large and spacious, and inside them bacon or herrings were often dried after salting. The majority of Snowdon cottages consisted of a single room in which the families both lived and slept, but sometimes a more developed variation– the *croglofft* (half-loft) were built. The walls were built of stone, and moss was used as rendering. The floor was earthern, occasionally covered with rushes, which were also used as bedding, as sometimes was hay. Around the cottages dry-stone walls were built.

Although no mortar or cement was used, they had to be solid enough to withstand the strong winds and storms on such exposed upland farms. The waller's art lay in his ability to work with irregular material of many sizes, and to size up each stone and then to judge how it would fit into a particular gap. Furthermore, the experienced waller didn't cut his materials to size if he could possibly help it, as the native stone was very hard, and therefore difficult to cleave cleanly.

Many of the cottages were located on the windy and rain-swept upland where it was important to have access to cattle and sheep at all times. For this reason, the long house that accommodated man and beast under the same roof was also commonplace.

As its name implies, such houses were single, long, low oblong buildings. The dwelling itself was always at one end, generally called the upper end (*pen uchaf*). The other, lower end (*pen isaf*) was the animal quarters. At a later date, the dwelling was often partitioned into two, three, or even four smaller rooms.

Large stones were used as tables and chairs, and also to fashion a hearth in which to burn peat and wood, the fire from which enabled food to be cooked, and gave heat to the room. Farmers living in the valleys and on the lower slopes, were often a little more civilised in that they sometimes had proper beds, and tables and chairs. However, they had few other comforts, and many still used the more sparsely furnished cottages on the higher slopes as *hafodau*, or summer cottages, whilst shepherding in the warmer months.

By the nineteenth century, some progress had been made, mainly in the valley farms. There the better weather conditions, better grazing land, and eventually, the influence of more modern farming techniques introduced by new farmers and landowners arriving from more affluent parts of Wales. Unfortunately, due to their attitudes and their lack of understanding of each other, they did little to help the mountain farmers who have now become almost an extinct race. One can still meet a farmer herding his animals on the land around the main paths, and they no longer rely totally on the harsh slopes of Snowdon to bring them a living.

So, when you're next on the summit of Snowdon, pause to reflect on the various early settlers and wonder which of these groups actually provided the first person to reach it. Might it have been a Celt hunting an animal for food, a Druid seeking a high position from which to atone the spirits, or even a stray legionnaire, lost in the frequently thick mists? What's more, are there any of them still there?

The Industries of Snowdon

Due to its geological formation, the land that makes up the Snowdon massif contains a large number of metals. Visitors to Snowdon therefore find that the industry that made the greatest impact on the mountain was copper mining, the most visual proof of this being Glaslyn (the blue lake) stained by the copper residues from the past. A lake which is almost 130 feet deep but in which no creature can live. Other remnants of the copper industry are also visible, especially from the Pig and Miners' Tracks.

The entrances to the various levels, the old mine buildings, and the positions of the tramways, are all remnants now, as the last mine finally closed in 1913. It was once thought that the copper industry had started in the eighteenth century. In fact this was merely a revival of an industry that had been prevalent in Roman times, and even before then – in pre-historic times – the tribes that settled on the shores of Llyn Llydaw used copper when making their bronze implements.

Copper mining was, however, only one of the industries that developed from the 'fruits' of this mountain. The other main industry was slate mining, and, as with the remnants of the copper industry, those of the slate industry, such as the old buildings and waste heaps, are to be found near both the Watkin and Rhyd-ddu paths.

When we talk about 'industries', we must bear in mind that until the eighteenth century, all the minerals and rocks extracted from Snowdon were mainly for domestic purposes. It was not until the industrial revolution that external demand occurred for slate for the buildings in the cotton towns of the north, and copper for the navy to 'copper-bottom' its ships. Other industries also drew products from Snowdon: chert (for the potteries), ochre (for paint making), calamine (for medicinal use), and manganese (for steel making) were all mined, but copper was the foremost industry, followed a close second by slate.

Opening to a copper mine above Glaslyn

The first copper mine actually on Snowdon (as opposed to being in Snowdonia) was at its base, in Llanberis. It was dug into the mountain just above Nant Peris, the original village of Llanberis, and employed between forty and fifty men, mainly from the local peasant farming community. Most of these miners never gave up being farmers and often used to take their sheep up to where they were mining, and allowed them to graze whilst they worked in the mine. In the summer months, even the miners' families helped to tend the sheep whilst they were underground. All that remains of the Llanberis mine now is the level at Clogwyn Goch, and ruins of the picking shed at Llyn Du'r Arddu.

Although the Llanberis copper mine was the first, the largest and best known was the Snowdon mine, the extensive levels of which penetrated the slopes above Glaslyn. This mine had a chequered history due in part to the fact that it was, at different times, owned by five different companies. The original owners were The Snowdon Copper Mining Company. Next was the Cwmdyli and Green Lake Copper Mining Company, which in turn sold it to The Great Snowdon Copper Mining Company. The next owner was The Great Snowdon Rock Company, and penultimately The Britannia Copper Mining Company – hence the other common name for the mine – The Britannia Mine. The last owners were The Penypass Copper Co. who took over in 1915, but were only to last a year – the mine ceased working in 1916.

In between the various companies that owned the mine, it was occasionally worked by individuals who acquired the lease but did not set up a company. Many of them made more of a success than the large companies. The mine was operated on what was called the 'bargain system', whereby a number of miners worked a specific part of the mine for a specific period, and paid the owners a percentage of the value of the ore mined, as rental, or lease. The company provided all the machinery that the miners required, and also arranged for the actual sale of the ore, but the miners themselves had to pay for both the gunpowder and the candles they needed in order to extract the ore from the mountain.

Initially, the ore was taken, usually by sledge, over the top of the mountain and down what is now the Snowdon Ranger Path from where it was taken to the coastal ports, although some was even taken in sacks on the backs of miners who used to climb a path from Glaslyn up the side of Clogwyn y Garnedd to Bwlch y Saethau. However, when Llanberis road was completed in 1832, it was much easier to transfer the ore by boat across Llyn Llydaw, and then by horse and cart to the top of the Llanberis Pass (Peny-pass), from where it was taken to Caernarfon.

Most of the levels of any significance were on the steep slopes between Glaslyn and the upper Pig Track where there were eight levels in total, all interconnected with box shoots, ladder-ways, and stopings (the steplike part of the mine where the ore was extracted). Most extended up to five hundred yards into the mountainside and although they now have surface water in their entrances, they are still quite dry inside because the levels were

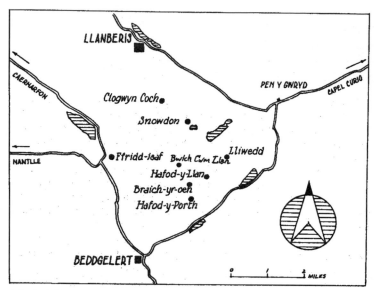

Fig 9. Mines and Quarries

always driven slightly uphill to drain them. It is interesting to note that a separate level which was dug immediately above the barracks at Glaslyn as a later addition to the mine, was the only level in which a steam drill was used to drill the blasting holes. The best vantage point from which to view the levels is from the Pig Track where the slope above Glaslyn comes into view. The brown stains caused by iron in the chalcopyrite (a compound of iron and copper) are clearly to be seen.

The first mine buildings above Glaslyn were originally a picking shed, stamps (the machinery that actually crushed the ore), and a waterwheel worked by water draining from the levels, but they have been derelict since before 1870. The major power-house on Snowdon was at the lip of Glaslyn, where the first waterwheel was built, powered by the stream leaving the lake. The wheel was built before the causeway, so the men who built it had to use boats to carry the parts of the 40 foot wheel to the site. The boats were flat-bottomed, capable of carrying twelve tons, and were pulled across the lake by ropes. They were also used to bring the materials with which to build a tramway around the lake to take the ore from the levels to the stamps.

46

The old mines at Lliwedd Bach

The old water wheel at Lliwedd Bach

The causeway across Llyn Llydaw was built by the Cwmdyli and Green Lake Company to ease the movement of men and equipment up to the mines. Originally, engineers planned to construct a road around the lake to prevent having to boat equipment and ore across the lake, which was a time consuming affair; prevented the most economical use of transport or horses; and restricted the size of machinery that could be installed. After studying the terrain the engineers concluded it would also be prohibitively expensive to build a tram-track around the lake, so suggested the causeway instead.

Construction was not a straightforward process. It would have been ineffective to dump mine waste into the water to form just a dam, because any structure would have to take a considerable amount of weight. The company's chief engineer – Captain Thomas Colliver – decided that the causeway had to be a more solid structure, and properly engineered.

In order to construct the causeway, he lowered the level of the lake twelve feet, which was done in two six foot stages that took nearly six months, and was completed on October 13th 1853. After the mines closed, the causeway was not maintained and became badly damaged, and was eventually re-built by the National Park wardens and Estate staff in 1978 and who now keep up the maintenance work. So the next time you walk across the causeway, just look around the edge of the lake, and try to imagine where the water level used to be. Only then can you really understand the problems the miners would have had to surmount, in trying to build a road around the lake, and what a task it is for the Wardens to keep the causeway in good condition.

The miners lot was not a very happy one, but they were the people who made most money from the Snowdon mine. Whenever the mine closed due to the failure of the company running it at that particular time, they knew from experience, that it would not be long before it was re-opened under new management, so the same miners came back each time. Most of the men came from Llanberis, travelling to work over Snowdon on a Monday morning, and returning the same way home on Saturday evening. Occasionally, men also came from Beddgelert to work at the main Snowdon mine, although the men from that village normally worked in the South Snowdon mines and quarries, usually because the employment was somewhat more secure, and because the mines were nearer to their homes.

The barracks of the Snowdon mine were erected during the harsh winter of 1801, with the miners having to dig through snowdrifts over 60 feet deep in some places. The ore from the mines was carried on the backs of miners up what is now known as the Miners' Track (the zig-zags) to Bwlch Glas where it was then put onto sledges drawn by horses, down to what was then the Saracen's Head (now the Snowdon Ranger) Path on the shore of Llyn Cwellyn, and then by cart to Caernarfon docks.

The Snowdon miners lived in barracks during the week and worked from eight in the morning until six at night. The first barracks were built at Teyrn in 1840, and were one room cottages. The barracks beside Glaslyn were built later, in 1873, when the Great Snowdon Mountain Copper Mining Company was established. The dressing floors where the miners worked were on the shores of Llyn Llydaw, and in their day were amongst the most modern copper mills in the country. The buildings consisted of a series of floors down which the ore, initially powered by gravity, passed through the various stages of refinement. Later, when the waterwheel at Glaslyn was fitted with a generator, the dressing floors ran off electricity.

At the top of the buildings, huge beams (which can still be seen in the ruins) supported the floor which held the Blake's crushers which were made of cast iron, each weighing about three tons. Below them were the hutchings, trammels, and Wifley tables. Outside the buildings were the round concrete circles of the self-acting buddles which then removed the last of the ore. Today, it is interesting to see the remnants of the Snowdon mining industry along the Miners' Track. The stone heap of 1854 and the cottages at Teyrn are still visible, and across the lake is the dark line where the inhabitants of the cottages cut their peat.

Between Llydaw and Glaslyn the series of man-made steps marking the track up which the miners carried the waterwheel, still exist. On the other side, leading from the stream that crosses the track, the series of supports, stone piles, and the place where the launder was can be seen. (The launder was the wooden trough that carried the water to the top of the dressing floors).

On the west shore of Glaslyn stand the ruins of a small building that stood alone. This was the gunpowder store, kept at a safe distance from the rest of the working machinery to prevent sparks getting to the contents. As a safety precaution, even the door handles were made of brass to prevent unwanted sparks. The pit in which the waterwheel turned is clearly seen at the lip of the lake, as are the remains of the oldest building, the smithy, where the drills for making blasting holes were sharpened. This might also be claimed to be the first cafe on Snowdon, as the smithy often sold cups of his tea to tourists.

But the mine at Glaslyn, although the most famous, was not the only one actually on Snowdon. Several other copper mines were to be found in the mountains north of Nant Gwynant, the main ones being Hafod-y-Porth, Lliwedd, Braich-Yr-oen, and Hafod-y-Llan, with the one at Lliwedd being the most productive (see Fig. 9). Braich-yr-Oen and Hafod-y-Llan often worked in conjunction, with the latter raising about 150 tons of copper (together with 30 tons of lead) in 1847. Alongside the waterfall at Lliwedd Bach was the mill consisting of waterwheels, roller crushers and associated dressing floors, and from it a stone-block railway led over a bridge across the river in the direction of Braich-Yr-oen. This mine eventually closed in 1886.

The mine at Hafod-y-Porth consisted of many workings that seem never to have rewarded the owners despite considerable investment and developments dating at least from 1755. In 1845, after owning it for a considerable time, The Bulkeley Mine Co. sold it, and even though a succession of other companies tried but failed to make it really profitable, the mine eventually faded into insignificance.

By walking up the Watkin Path (the old cart track to the south Snowdon quarries, the remnants of these three mines can be seen. On the left just before the swing gate is the mine's incline, and across the river where the track comes close to the cascading Afon Cwm Llan is the old mine's path with steps formed of large stone flags leading up to the Hafod-y-Llan mill with the ruins of the large wheelpit and crusher house.

On the mountainside to the right are the workings and levels of Hafod-y-Llan, from which a narrow-gauge tramway conveyed the ore along an embankment before passing down a slide to the mill which was powered by the water from the river. Over the base of the slope up to Yr Aran, the remains of the mill and other buildings of Hafod-y-Porth can be seen.

The Lliwedd mine was situated high up in Cwm Merch, and consisted of crevasse-like opencuts. A cart-track leads up to the old crusher-house into which the ore was fed from a steep stone-lined shoot at the top of which lay the tramline. In fact some of the old rusting trams can still be seen there. Higher up are spectacular but dangerous vertical openings alongside which can be seen the extensive waste-tips. The old crushing mill is in ruins but pieces of the original waterwheel can still be seen lying around, as can the old stamp-heads and rolls.

The other copper mine that was nearest to the summit was the Clogwyn Coch mine close to Llyn Du'r Arddu, which was opened towards the end of the eighteenth century. It shared its workers with the mines at Llanberis, and the workers would work at Clogwyn in the summer, and Llanberis in the winter. It was thought at one stage that Snowdon and Clogwyn had inter-connecting passages, but this has never been confirmed.

The mine at Llanberis which was opened in the middle of the eighteenth century, was part of the Faenol Estate and was highly productive. It consisted of four main areas of activity – Lower Works, Yew Tree Works, Smithy Works, and Bridge Works. The main method of transporting the ore from the mine was by boat across Llyn Peris and then via horse drawn sledges to Caernarfon. The mine closed in 1885, and most of the workings have now been obliterated by the new hydro-electric storage scheme.

It is worth remembering though, that not all the mining on Snowdon was carried out on such a grand scale as the mines just described. There are leases listed in record books of the area, that showed many one-man ventures, all set on making their fortune from the ore rich ground, though none really succeeding. Such leases were for a specific area of land on which the tennant could dig, and the remnants of these amateur mines can be seen by the heaps of stones and small holes found in the area. I suppose that for about fifty shillings a year rent, it was worth the risk of having a go!

The other southern mines yielded slate, of which the most visable is at Cwm y Llan, and can be reached by a track from Rhyd-ddu. The Bwlch Cwm y Llan quarry drew its workforce mainly from Beddgelert, the men travelling to work via the track through Gwernlas Deg. Other large deposits of mine tips can also be seen from the Snowdon Ranger Path when looking towards

Rhyd-ddu. It must be emphasised however, that not only must permission be obtained to visit any of these remains (as they are all on private land), but also the ruins themselves are very dangerous places and should not be entered.

In comparison with the copper industry, the slate industry of Snowdon was very backward, development proceeding slowly. Indeed in 1832 the output was 100,000 tons, only rising by 1882 to 450,000 tons. But by 1972, the output was a mere 22,000 tons, and whereas Welsh slate was once known as 'common slate', it eventually became increasingly uncommon. Now, concrete and tiles have replaced what was once a universal roofing material.

The word 'slate' is derived from the late Middle English word 'slat' or 'sclate'; but after about 1630 the form with 'scl' or 'ski' became exclusive to Scotland. The word slate is also connected with the French verb 'escalter' – to break into pieces – referring to the substance's characteristic property of splitting into thin sheets. In Wales, the words *ysglatus*, *ysglats* and *sglatys* were commonly used for slate, all derived from a fifteenth-century term.

The geological definition of slate rests on the type of 'cleavage' (in Welsh – *hollt*) which means that the slate can be split into strong, even sheets of almost any size, in a direction unrelated to the bedding planes (see geology chapter), and central Gwynedd (including Snowdon) is one of five areas in Wales where slate of commercial importance can be found, due to the slate beds of the Cambrian Age. These beds stretch from Bethesda via Llanberis and Nantlle to Penygroes, and include those of one of the largest slate quarries in the world – Dinorwig – on the slope of Elidir Fawr, overlooking the Llanberis Pass. But there were also some smaller mines on the Rhyd-ddu side of Snowdon too.

There is a great deal of variation in the colour of the slates, even in an individual quarry. In the Llanberis area they can be divided into 'green – vein', 'curly red', old 'blue vein', 'hard spotted blue vein', 'royal blue vein', 'curly red vein', 'red hard vein' and 'Glynrhonwy vein'.

The slate industry didn't exist in an organised form until the second half of the eighteenth century , but there is evidence that slate has been used for roofing since Roman times. It is probable also that slates were used as bakestones from medieval times, especially to bake the flat, inch thick bread known as *bara llech*, or 'slate bread', and it is thought that this type of baking was continued until the introduction of iron bakestones in around 1780.

Slate did not become a universal roofing material in Wales until the nineteenth century. Before then most small dwellings, and also some churches had thatched roofs, because builders depended largely on local materials being available, as slate was a heavy material and was expensive to transport. These transportation costs were also a deciding factor on the closure of a number of Snowdon mines such as Hafod-y-Llan, and the South Snowdon Slate Quarry , especially as the quality of the slate mined was not always worth the effort, and there was often a high proportion of waste.

In 1843 a tramway was planned from the Snowdon slate quarries to Porthmadog, but this never materialised, mainly due to the fact that the landowners on the proposed route could not be persuaded to sell their land, but also because the output of the mines couldn't have really made the project cost-effective.

There were a number of small mines on the outskirts of the Snowdon massif, such as Bryn Mawr and Bwlch-y-Groes both closed in 1928; Caermeinciau closed in 1900; Gallt-y-Llan closed in 1946; Upper Glynrhonwy, Goodman and Cambrian also closed in 1930; and Cook and Ddol closed in 1937; all based around Llanberis. Also Bwlch-y-Ddwyelor closed in 1890, and Glanrafon closed in 1914, both near Rhyd-ddu. But the main slate quarries of the Snowdon area were those on the opposite sides of Elidir Fawr – Dinorwig on the Llanberis side which closed in the 1960s and Penrhyn on the Nant Ffrancon side, but neither really true Snowdon quarries in the terms of this book. The only true quarries were the Snowdon quarry, closed in 1882, and Hafod-y-Llan – or South Snowdon quarry – which closed in 1880.

One industry in Snowdon still in operation, was the last one to arrive: hydroelectricity. Since they were started, all the mines and quarries used water as their source of power, but with the advent of electricity in the late nineteenth century, the mine's original waterwheels were adapted to generate this new-found and much more adaptable power source. With other industries being developed in the area surrounding Snowdon, it didn't take long to

The pipeline in Cwm Dyli

realise the huge potential of the natural supply of water there as a source of hydro-electricity, and in 1903 the North Wales Power and Traction Company was formed (under statutory powers) to do just this.

The power was to be generated from a power-station at the base of Cwm Dyli which would use Llyn Llydaw as headwater. To transport the water from Llydaw to the power-station, a pipeline had to be made. Documentation shows that the method used to transport the sections of pipes up Cwm Dyli was the water from the stream that the pipes were eventually to replace. Inclines powered by water-filled counter wagons pulleyed the pipe sections up, and they were then joined together. Unfortunately, the engineers of the day either didn't have the foresight, or technical expertise to make it an underground one; the monstrous eyesore is still in existence today (see image on following page).

Even worse was the huge number of transmission lines inevitably required to transport the electricity. For many years, arguments and even court cases arose over them. In 1927 questions were even raised in Parliament concerning the 'disfiguration of Snowdonia', but it was not until Snowdonia became a National Park that action was taken to remove them.

It is a shame that after all the years of industry on Snowdon, the one that remains the greatest eyesore is that of the most modern – the Cwm Dyli pipeline. The ruins of the Glaslyn mines, the workings on the shores of Llyn Llydaw, even the tips in Cwm Tregalan, all exude a feeling of nostalgia, and thoughts of the hardship that must have been part of the everyday life of the men that worked there. There is no such empathy for the engineers of the hydro-electric industry. Now, the only other industry on Snowdon is the mountain railway, which is more of a leisure industry than anything.

The Snowdon Mountain Railway

The possibility of laying a railway track to the summit of Snowdon was discussed for many years, but it wasn't until 1871 that a Bill was presented to Parliament to incorporate a company to do so. However, the Bill had to be withdrawn because the owner of the land at that time – George William Duff Assheton Smith, the squire of the Faenol Estate – would not give his support. He felt that a railway would scar the landscape, and not bring any tangible benefits to the village of Llanberis, where the station was planned. In some ways this suited the people of Beddgelert, who wanted their village to be the base for mountaineering on Snowdon. Assheton Smith's view did not agree however with the majority of the population of Llanberis, nor indeed with the many small-holders living on the slopes of Snowdon on his estate. They were conscious of the fact that Llanberis needed some form of activity to encourage the tourist trade that was being seen in nearby villages.

Llanberis thrived on both the slate trade and its seasonal influx of visitors arriving from Caernarfon on the LNWR line. But in 1822, following the success of the Ffestiniog Railway, the North Wales Narrow Gauge Railway Co. was formed with the intention of constructing a railway link between Porthmadog and Betws-y-coed, via Beddgelert. A further line was also planned from Dinas (on the LNWR line between Caernarfon and Afon Wen) to Tryfan and the slate quarries at Bryngwyn, with a branch from Tryfan to Rhyd-ddu – just three miles from the summit of Snowdon. Plans for the former were eventually abandoned but the latter line was commenced in 1876.

The track quickly advanced eastwards from Dinas Junction (or Llanwnda Junction as it was originally known) towards Snowdon and down along its western flank. Passenger traffic began in August 1877 from Dinas Junction to Cwellyn Station at the northern end of Llyn Cwellyn. In June of the following year the service was extended further to Snowdon Ranger on the

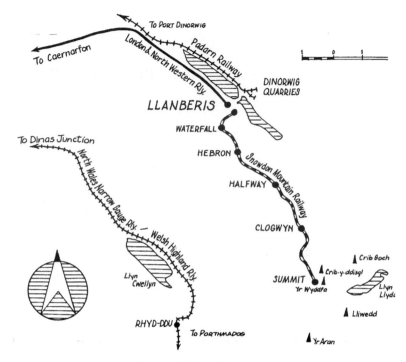

Fig. 10. The Industrial Railways of Snowdon

eastern shore of the lake, and the final extension to Rhyd-ddu was opened in May 1881.

Initially, the line's potential for tourist traffic was not fully realised and both the terminus at Rhyd-ddu and the railway itself began slowly to decay. In 1894, the NWNGR then hit upon the innovative idea of changing the name of the station to 'Snowdon' station, and although slightly misleading (it was over three miles from Snowdon's summit) the name proved effective, attracting many travellers. With the new name, the NWNGR experienced a marked change in its turnover, and Llanberis started to feel the effects. The village had for years relied on its proximity to Snowdon, and now this was being challenged.

In 1894 when the North Wales Narrow Gauge Railway changed the name of Rhyd-ddu Station to Snowdon Station, the villagers of Llanberis became even more discontented. A further deputation visited Assheton Smith at Faenol and again pointed

SNOWDON TRAIN ON VIADUCT, LLANBERIS. W.1567.

Train on a viaduct

out that Beddgelert was viewed as the main focal point of tourism in Snowdonia at the expense of Llanberis and the Faenol Estate, and eventually he succumbed. In November of that year, a new company – The Snowdon Mountain Tramroad and Hotels Co Ltd – was formed, and the necessary land was purchased from the Faenol Estate, which also agreed to rent the Royal Victoria Hotel as part of the deal.

The task ahead of the new company was quite daunting. The landscape it had purchased was very exposed, very rocky and in some parts extremely steep. One should also remember that in those days there were no mechanical diggers or tracked vehicles so all the machinery required for the project had to be transported on horse-drawn sledges. Furthermore, the task was not just simply laying a track. Five stations had to be built and, even more difficult, two viaducts were required to span the River Hwch near the base station at Llanberis.

It was eventually agreed that the main system to be used for the railway was the Abt one (named after Dr Roman S. Abt, a Swiss engineer). It was based on using steel bars that had teeth mechanically cut on the upper part of them, which when laid side by side, allowed the teeth to alternate with each other, thus providing a constant connection between the pinions on the train,

Padarn at Llanberis Station

and the teeth on the track below. This prevented the train slipping on inclines, and provided a smooth ride overall. The track gauge was the same as that found on some of the European lines of the same type – 800mm (2 feet 7½ inches).

The men working on the railway lived and slept in wooden huts built specifically for the purpose. After a working week of six days they took Sunday off. The first phase of the project was to erect the two viaducts across the River Hwch in order that trains could then take machinery to where it was required further up the track. The methods of construction used for the earthworks were those in common use at that time with the navvies employing their traditional tools of picks, shovels, and wheelbarrows. For wielding these they received 6½d per hour, and out of this 1½d was a 'height money' bonus. The more skilled workers such as the masons employed on the viaducts received 8½d per hour with a height bonus of 2d.

When one considers how workmen are helped by technology today, what with excavators, power drills and even helicopters to transport machinery to remote places, the men who built the Snowdon railway really were Trojans. After the earthworks and the viaducts had been completed, the whole track (almost five

Approaching the summit

miles in length) was laid in just seventy-two working days – an average of 1,200 yards a day. Until the first two engines arrived all they had were horse-drawn sledges, so one can only imagine what they might have achieved with modern machinery. It is also interesting to note that even after the arrival of the engines, the shirehorses were still used to reach remoter parts. Perhaps I am a romantic, but I think I would have preferred to see the beauty of Daylight and Strawberry (two of the Shires), rather than the metal locomotives Enid and Ladas.

Whilst there was general support for the building of the railway from the inhabitants of Llanberis and other neighbouring villages, there were still some who condemned the venture. One person in particular was Canon H.O. Rawnsley who, as well as being a respected priest, was also the honourary secretary to the National Trust for the Preservation of Historic and Natural Beauty. He felt, as did many of his followers, that not only would the railway be an eyesore, but it could be the start of a series of such railways to the summit of other mountains not only in north. Wales, but also elsewhere in Great Britain.

In the many letters distributed at that time, there emerged pertinent arguments both for and against the railway's existence.

The summit station

Some felt that thousands of young and old people who might not be fit enough to walk to the top could at least enjoy the views currently experienced by just a few climbers. Others felt that the mountain was among the few places in which solitude could be found even in that period, and that it should remain that way.

Now the summit is crowded in the summer months, and it is only at dawn or on a bleak January day that any solitude can be found, although one must be mindful that for every one person that arrives at the summit by train, it is estimated that a further three walk there. Furthermore, although some people feel that the benefits from the railway that were originally meant for the village of Llanberis have not really materialised, without the railway over seventy employees in the village would be without a job.

The ceremony of officially cutting the first sod took place on Saturday 15th December 1894 by G.W. Duff Assheton Smith and his six year old daughter Enid. At lunch later in the nearby Royal Victoria Hotel, it was pointed out that villagers should benefit from the increased tourism that the railway would bring, but were warned not to overcharge them for various local services, as they would tell their friends not to come to Llanberis!

After very bad weather at the beginning of 1895, a progress

report in the spring of that year predicted that the opening of the railway would not be possible on the day originally planned, July 1st. However, despite the severe weather, the team of over 150 men had cleared over two and a half miles of track by the end of March. In the April of 1895, the team was increased to over 200 men, to catch up on the time lost due to the winter conditions, which they eventually did, having laid approximately 8,500 sleepers on the track between the base and summit stations.

On 23rd May the subscription list of the company's shares was opened, the issue was of 6,343 shares at £10 each, and mortgage debentures of £100 each. The first subscriber was a Mrs Alice May Corbett of Wrexham, and apart from those purchased by the directors of the Railway Company, and of the companies involved in the railway's construction, most of the other shares were bought by individuals from outside the locality.

By June, most of the track was ready but there was considerable work remaining to be done on the seven bridges, two viaducts and the various cuttings, so the 1st July opening was postponed. Later that month, the first locomotive arrived from Switzerland and was named 'Ladas' in honour of Laura Alice Duff Assheton Smith. It was given the Number 1, and even today, employees of the railway still refer to it by number as they do to all the engines. Only the passengers refer to them by their names.

Work continued to progress well, and at three minutes to eleven on Thursday, 9th January 1896, the first train to reach the summit left Llanberis Station. It didn't carry passengers, just a number of company officials and workmen on a test run to check the track. The journey was successful, but there still remained some work to be done on the station buildings, and also the large amount of fencing. The delay during construction meant that the railway had lost the opportunity of being the first mountain railway in the British Isles, for on the 21st August 1895, the Snaefell Mountain Railway on the Isle of Man was officially opened to the public.

The next complete journey was undertaken on 27th March, when the Chief Inspector of the Board of Trade in London visited the railway. As the railway was a private venture it was not a legal necessity to have the system checked prior to an official approval, but the Chief Inspector was known to one of the consultant engineers. The only major recommendations he made were that a buffer was needed at the summit until the station had been completed, a second platform was advisable at Hebron, and that trains should have restricted running when wind pressure reached 15 lbs per square foot – or 68 m.p.h. – hurricane force.

To assist the latter, a machine was installed at Clogwyn Station to measure wind speed. In fact many villagers of Nant Peris collected an assortment of hats over the years when low-sided carriages were used, as the strong winds frequently blew the hats of passengers down into the valley. The valley was eventually known by the locals as 'Cwm Retia' (hat valley), and is even sometimes named so on OS maps. The earliest carriages each seated fifty passengers on wooden seats, and were open-sided to prevent the high winds of Clogwyn blowing the carriages off the track. Today, all the carriages have side panels, doors and glass windows.

Despite a slight accident when a carriage came off the line during one of the final test stages on 4th April, it was decided that the railway should open to the public on Easter Monday, 6th April, 1896, after a total expenditure of £76,000. Easter Monday was a superb spring day, sunny with blue skies. Workers set off at daylight to inspect the complete length of the track and they were followed by a team on a 'pilot' train. Both teams reported that everything was in order, and that the official opening could commence later in the day. The directors had decided that there was no need for an official opening ceremony. Even so quite a large crowd gathered to see the first train leave Llanberis Station. It is believed that 'Enid' was the engine that made the inaugural journey on which about eighty fare paying passengers participated. 'Ladas' left afterwards and both engines reached the summit safely.

However, on the return journey, when Ladas was on the steepest part of the track – about one hundred yards from the bridge that crosses the public footpath above Clogwyn Station – the engine lost connection with the track and hurtled down the track at an uncontrollable speed. 'Ladas' left the track on the bend above Cwm Glas Bach and plunged down the cliffs into the cwm.

Because the carriages were – and are still – not coupled to the engines, Mr Gowrie Aitchinson, the Railway's Manager, who was travelling in the first carriage, was able to apply the carriage's brakes and stop the rest of the train. But as 'Ladas' fell into the cwm, it hit the trackside telegraph poles and cables causing a short circuit to occur which inadvertently rang the bell at the summit station which was the signal for the train there to leave. As it had now become very misty on the mountain, 'Enid''s driver took extreme caution and started the journey at the slowest possible speed. However, he could not prevent his train crashing into the stationary carriages at Clogwyn, but all the carriages were fortunately pushed into the passing loop, where they came to a halt.

The early engines did not have speedometers. The drivers had to use their experience and judgement as to the speed they went. Now some of the engines are fitted with them. Each engine, though, has brakes of three varieties: handbrakes, steam and counter pressure. The latter is used on the downward journey as there is no steam produced. The brakes systems of the carriages act independently from those of the engines. Furthermore although not used today, the track originally had signals at the base and summit stations and at various places on the track where trains were likely to pass each other. They were removed in 1933 and the railway now uses the 'permissive ticket' system to ensure that two trains are not on the same section of track at the same time.

Except for one, all the passengers escaped injury after the accident and were able to walk back to Llanberis. The only one hurt was a Mr Ellis Roberts, the proprietor of the local Padarn Villa Hotel, who tried to jump for safety when he saw the driver and the fireman of 'Ladas' doing likewise. Unfortunately he sustained serious injuries, had to have one of his legs amputated, and died later that night. He was buried in Nant Peris Cemetery. At the inquest that followed the accident, it was generally agreed that the cause of the accident was due to ice, that had formed under the rails, melting in the sunlight and thus causing the foundations of the track to slip, leaving the inner part over two inches lower than the outer.

By the end of April the track had been repaired but it was not until the summer that safety rails had been placed along the side of the track. In August, another engine, aptly named 'Snowdon' arrived from Switzerland, and by September some trains were running again as far as the Waterfall Station (now no longer used). The winter of 1896-7 was a very hard one and the track on the high slopes was under six feet of snow until well into spring but, on Easter Monday 1897, a train with railway staff on board set out to check the track and it was agreed that the railway could be officially re-opened, which it was later that day, exactly one year after the crash. By the end of the year, over 12,000 passengers had travelled to the summit. In 2005, that figure had multiplied to over 140,000 a year.

The railway continued its service into the early 1900s, and even in the First World War, the service was uninterrupted, though restricted at some times. In the late 1920s and early 1930s several major internal changes took place within the SMT&H Co, the most obvious of these being the change of name in 1928 to the more succinct – Snowdon Mountain Railway Ltd. The SMR went from strength to strength and it soon became obvious that the NWNGR hardly constituted a serious threat to the Snowdon Railway, especially since its terminus was a good three-and-a-half mile walk from the summit. Attempts were continually being made to complete the original planned NWNGR scheme, but these failed, and in October 1916, the daily service between Dinas Junction and Snowdon ceased.

However, in March 1922, the Welsh Highland Railway (Light Railway) Co. was incorporated, with the necessary powers to take over the old concern, and re-open the Dinas-Porthmadog link. The old NWNGR section was reconditioned and re-opened for passenger traffic as far as Snowdon Station, now renamed once again, this time as South Snowdon.

Work continued on the link section and the first passengers travelled to Porthmadog in June 1923, but unfortunately it was too late to save the railway. The new road systems in north Wales were now allowing travellers to reach the area by car or other means of transport, which left the Welsh Highland railway to cater more for the railway enthusiasts rather than those that could have made it a commercial success. Even after a number of new ownerships and some extra income from goods traffic, the line closed in 1941 leaving the Snowdon Mountain Railway as being the only vehicular way to the summit.

Even World War Two had no dramatic effect on the operation of the railway. Between 1940 and 1944 a restricted public service ran whilst the Ministry of Supply carried out experimental radio work at the summit and the Air Ministry requisitioned the summit hotel for important radar development work. The hotel also came under control of the Admiralty whilst further secret work was being carried out, but the railway reopened to the public again in May 1945.

Unfortunately, one effect of the war on the railway was that it suffered from neglect and poor maintenance as a result of a shortage of both men and materials, and a great deal of repair work was required to bring it up to safe public safety standards again. In the 1950s and 1960s therefore many improvements were made resulting in better amenities and conditions. Most of the coaching stock was rebuilt and the old semi-open coaches were converted into more modern closed carriages, one of the seven being completed each year. At the same time, the structure of the summit hotel was also improved. In fact, it was whilst these repairs were being undertaken that the most serious accident ever to happen on Snowdon took place. In what was considered some of the worst weather for years, an RAF Anson aircraft on a flight from Northern Ireland crashed into the mountain close to the Clogwyn Coch rock-face in August 1952, scattering burning wreckage over the track that one of the trains had just passed, and preventing the other from descending. The three crew unfortunately died, and the railway was closed, leaving the passengers stranded in the summit 'hotel' until the next day. To this day, the bend on the line where the Anson crashed, is called 'Tro Eroplen' – Aeroplane Bend.

In 1960, modernisation work commenced at the line's lower terminus with the enlarging and refitting of the station shop and modernisation of the restaurant, thus attracting many more visitors. At the same time a period of intensive repairs was started on the engines, and after being taken out of service in 1939, the engine Snowdon was eventually steamed again in 1963. There are now seven engines used in rotation. They are listed here with the numbers allocated to them, and the date in which they arrived at Llanberis:

No 2 – Enid (1895)
No 3 – Wyddfa (1895)
No 4 – Snowdon (1896)
No5 – Moel Siabod(1896)
No 6 – Padarn (1922)
No 7 – Ralph (1923)
No 8 – Eryri (1923)

'Padarn' was originally called 'Sir Harmood' after the first Chairman, and 'Ralph' was called 'Aylwin', but is now named after R. Sadler, one of the consulting engineers. In 1986 two diesel engines were acquired:

No 9 – Ninian – named after a Chairman: Ninian Davies.
No 10 – Yeti – a name chosen by children in a national TV competition(dedicated to all creatures of mountains).

In 1991 a further diesel locomotive was purchased, No 11, named 'Peris', and the following year No 12, 'George', was added. In 1995 the Railway took delivery of three diesel-electric railcars capable of multiple unit operation, manufactured in South Wales by HPE Tredegar Ltd. Each unit is capable of being coupled with one or two other units for multiple unit operation, still under the control of a single driver and guard.

During the hour long journey, a locomotive also uses an average of seven hundredweight of coal, which was formerly obtained from the south wales coalfield but which is now imported from Poland. The diesel engines use around 70 litres on a return journey.

There are five stations on the line, Llanberis (base); Hebron; Halfway; Clogwyn; and the Summit. At one time, the trains used to stop at the Waterfall Station too, but they now only slow down for passengers to take photographs. There is also a small platform at Rocky Valley just below Clogwyn, which is the furthest point to which trains venture if the weather is very bad.

Waiting at the Clogwyn passing point

Hebron (at 930 feet) was named due to its proximity to Hebron Chapel, home in the past of a thriving community, and which made a station commercially viable.

Halfway (1,614 feet) consists of a small hut and a reservoir which holds 9,000 gallons, filled from a pipe coming from an overflow at Clogwyn. Over 100 gallons of water are required on the journey to the summit. The older engines have to take on extra supplies at this station, whereas more modern ones have larger capacity tanks enabling them to reach the summit without refilling. Just below the station, on the Llanberis Path, is the Halfway Hut where walkers can obtain light refreshments during the summer months.

Clogwyn (at 2541 feet) is the most exposed station but also has the most spectacular views down the Llanberis Pass. It is named after the famous rock-climbing cliffs of Clogwyn Du'r Arddu.

At the Summit station (3543 feet – the summit cairn is at 3560) food and drinks are available usually between mid May and mid October, when staff live in residents' accommodation at the station. Between these times (when shelter and hot food and drinks are really most required!) it is unfortunately closed and barricaded. This is because the trains are unable to reach the summit because of bad weather conditions, so essential services cannot be maintained. However the barricades are the result of the problems of modern day living when vandals manage to venture even to this wild spot.

The Summit

The first man-made structure built on the summit of Snowdon was a wall running across the top, acting as the boundary between the Baron Hill Estate on the south, and the Faenol Estate on the north. This was in the early eighteenth century , and there were references made to it by both Pennant and Bingley in their travel books. However, the first building that could be used for accommodation was a circular shelter with a roof that looked very much like a beehive, which was built by William Lloyd the Beddgelert guide around about 1815, using some of the stones from the original wall. It was used mainly by climbers to shelter from the elements, or to stay overnight to watch the sunsets, and was called, appropriately, Snowdon Cottage.

The next structure to be built on the summit was the cairn, the first one being erected in 1827 by the Royal Engineers as part of a national ordnance survey, and was merely an ordinary pile of stones used to support their measuring instruments. This cairn was replaced in 1841 by the much larger one that is often shown in photographs and drawings of that time. Around this time another item was placed on the summit – a pole eighteen feet high which was itself on top of a pile of stones fifteen feet high. This became one of the most famous landmarks of the summit, and until well into the late 1880s many people climbed it to write their names as near as possible to the top!

The excellent idea of providing refreshments on the summit of Snowdon belongs to a miner, who was at that time working in Clogwyn Coch copper mine. He was Morris Williams, from Amlwch, in Anglesey, and it was whilst busily engaged in the mine that it occurred to him that a large number of visitors climbed Snowdon during the summer months, and perhaps it would pay him to provide a small hut near the summit where they might get something to refresh themselves. He tried the experiment once or twice without the hut, taking with him tea, coffee, butter, bread, and cheese, and was soon convinced that a living could be made.

The first hut was built about 1837 or 1838, and was situated below the summit cairn, on the property of Hafod-y-Llan. Its outer walls were of stone, and its inner lining of neatly planed boards. The buildings that could have been described as 'hotels' weren't built until around 1840. These were two huts, built for the owners of the Royal Victoria Hotel in Llanberis, and built by the men who worked in the copper mine at Llyn Du'r Arddu. The first of the huts initially had a reputation for being a Temperance Inn, but this soon changed, and by the time the second hut had been built, both were dispensing alcoholic beverages. The huts had beds, seating furniture, fires for cooking and warmth, and provided hot meals for visitors. But it is probably for their visitor books that they are now famous. These provided a marvellous account of life on the summit between 1845 and 1889, and contained many details about the weather, poems written by visitors, details of the various routes up, remarks about the food and drink, and many claims about the first climbs on some of the rock-faces.

Other remarks left in the visitor books were more related to the problems that occurred caused by the ever increasing number of people reaching the summit. For example, one visitor wrote:

> Our party of twelve is spending the night here. Some of them are asleep, sound as a pig and sprawling all over the floor, apparently in Elysium. I have just looked out. The wind is blowing great guns and the fog is thick. I am footsore, sleepy and cold and I expect to be wet to the skin on my descent. 3 am. 9/10 August 1848.

Another visitor not only described some of the problems but also at the same time gave a concise description of life at one of the huts:

> Many persons will be disappointed in the Peak of Yr Wyddfa in not being able to enjoy the solitude so dear to a mountaineer. On the top is a large cairn close by which have been built three rude huts where a man and his wife live during the whole of summer. They provide tea, beer, eggs, bread, butter and cheese and accommodate visitors with bedrooms and small sitting rooms and fires where they remain overnight

The summit in Edwardian times

The train arrives in the shadow of the summit hotel

and see the sunrise. The charge is eight shillings for supper, bed and breakfast, one shilling for a bottle of beer, and two shillings for a single meal. It is advisable not only to see the sunrise but also to see it set which is generally the more beautiful. Of course the traveller will often meet with disappointment at the top. It is not unusual for it to be in dense mist on many successive days.

Not all the entries in the visitors books were derogatory; in fact some were very humorous, some were poetic, some visitors 'of the cloth' even wrote sermons, but none could beat the entry by a Mr Charles Edwards in 1845 who claimed:

I have not been idle since I came here. I have composed an essay and two poems, one in English one in Welsh, written three letters but could not find a post office, engraved my name on the plank on the summit, collected five or six plants and several stones, read two pamphlets and a chapter from the Bible, sang ten hymns and two anthems, talked on various subjects to my young companions, ate eggs, bread and bacon, drank tea and coffee which were exceedingly good, paid my fare to the kind landlord and shall descend at twelve noon.

After the arrival of the railway, there were eventually five buildings on the summit, and by the late nineteenth century, they could no longer really be described as 'huts'. They were larger than the original huts – one being nearly thirty-five feet by fifteen feet.

The arrival of the railway was also responsible for the conflicts between the various people laying claim to land on the summit, especially those with huts there. As was mentioned earlier, the original wall that was built on the summit divided the Baron Hill and Faenol Estates. However Sir Edward Watkin (of Watkin Path) had his suspicions about the position of the boundaries especially in relation to the position of the huts.

When the huts were initially built, they were small and had been built on land leased from the Faenol Estate. In the 1890s, they were bigger and had spread onto land which he claimed was his. Furthermore, when they were originally built, the owners of the huts were not using them on a commercial basis, but with the trade being brought to the summit by the railway, the huts were worth a much greater value. Eventually, proper agreements were made with the parties concerned, and the Railway Company then added their terminus too, and by 1898, the Company had taken over the sole possession of the summit. The only non-Company trader was Mr James Leach, a photographer from Llanberis, who took photos of visitors on the summit and had a small hut there in which to develop his plates.

After this period, many plans were drawn up for 'hotels' on the summit and by the early 1900s there was a chalet-style building there in which many club functions were held, in carpeted rooms with proper furniture and fixtures. In fact an advertisement by the Snowdon Mountain Tramroad Company announced that 'The Highest Hotel in the Kingdom' had been 'Newly Furnished Throughout' and that "Visitors who desire to see one of the grandest sights in the world, should ascend Snowdon in the evening and stay the night to witness the Sunrise over the Snowdonian Range".

In 1922, plans were drawn up for a new station terminus and hotel – to be built into the mountain, but the company couldn't afford to build it. Instead, in 1923, just the new station was built, and as part of this development, after many years faithful service to the climbing fraternity, the old huts were demolished. However, just twelve years later, this station too was further developed by Sir Clough Williams-Ellis, the creator of Portmeirion, and in 1935 the building is now being replaced was completed.

As we have seen, the summit building lost its public hotel status during the Second World War. From 1942-1945 it was requisitioned by the Ministry of Supply for experimental radio work, then by the Air Ministry for radar development. Next, the Admiralty carried out secret work there and finally the Army had use of it.

After the war, the hotel rooms were used, as they are now, to accommodate the staff who work on the summit, many of whom live there from May to September. For many years the hotel was left open during the winter months so that climbers could shelter in it in extreme weather conditions, but after extensive vandalism in 1951, the company decided to close it during the winter months, and as anyone who has visited the summit on a bleak January day will know, it's not much fun having to stand outside, when there could be warmth within.

Despite improvements carried out in 1952-54 and some additions in 1968, the summit building showed signs of serious wear and tear from the enormous pressures placed upon it from the modern day tourism it had not been built to withstand. Such pressures were largely responsible for a radical change in thinking regarding the public access to the summit. So when large areas of Snowdon came up for sale in 1968, they were bought by the Secretary of State for Wales and then sold to the tenants on condition that they entered into Access Agreements with the National Park Authority, allowing free public access to the open mountain provided certain byelaws were respected.

In the early 1970s a team of consultants also looked at the issues facing the summit of Snowdon from tourism, and after the report was published, a five-year Snowdon Management Scheme was launched. Under the guidance of the National Park Authority and with a grant from the Countryside Commission, gangs of workers repaired the badly eroded footpaths up to the summit. Furthermore, the consultants' survey also showed that more than half the users of the summit building were walkers rather than train passengers, and the National Park Authority felt some obligation towards the Railway Company to help out with much needed refurbishment. After complex negotiation, it was decided that the most practical solution would be for the Park Authority to purchase the building from the Railway Company (in order that grants from public bodies could be more readily available), which they did in 1982, and then leased the building back to the Railway Company, which still manages it.

In June 2002, the Snowdonia Park Authority resolved to accept a design by architects Furneaux Stewart as the basis for a new building for the summit. It would include a warden presence, first aid station, centre for weather information, orientation and descent advice, washrooms and toilets in addition to refreshments and shelter. Visitors of all ages and abilities would have the opportunity to learn more about the mountain's significance as a unique recreational, environmental and cultural resource.

However, following detailed consultation with relevant organi-sations, it was suggested that including a winter refuge within the design would encourage people to be over ambitious in attempting to reach the summit. The British Mountaineering Council and Local Mountain Rescue Teams advised that a shelter would cause problems in this respect, so yet again, when experienced walkers need it most, there will be no adequate shelter on the summit.

In January 2004 planning permission was granted and during the following month it was announced that work would begin in 2006, the completed building to be ready by summer 2008, at an estimated cost of £10,000,000, most of which would be in the form of grants from organisations such as the Wales Tourist Board, the Welsh Development Agency, Snowdon Mountain Railway, Gwynedd Economic Partnership and the Welsh Assembly Government. The Snowdonia National Park Authority has also reserved funds for the project.

The toughest challenge for both the construction of the build-ing and its future operation will come from the weather. The average rainfall on Snowdon is 200 inches per year, and the temperature varies from 30°C in the summer to -20°C in the winter, but as the wind can reach speeds of 150 mph, the cooling effect can often reduce the temperature by a further 30°C. What's more, the summit is often covered by frost or snow from November right through until April. But for me, one of the best memories of my life will be seeing dawn from the summit, and this I recommend every serious lover of this great mountain should experience once in their lifetime.

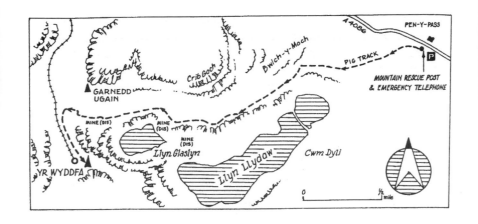

The Pig Track Route

The Pig or Pyg Track is almost 3 miles long and starts at Pen-y-pass. The first stage is to Bwlch-y-moch (the pass of pigs) from which the path supposedly takes its name. The alternative name PYG was in theory given to it by the habitués of the Penygwryd Hotel in the early 1900s, though some sources say it was derived from *pyg* the Welsh word for the pitch used in the copper mines, and hence the route used to get it to them. It starts in a westerly direction from the car park at Pen-y-pass through a gap in the stone wall under the high power cables, and is quite well marked.

For most of the way the route is over boulders and scree as the path meanders over very rough ground, and at one part passes through a series of enormous boulders before entering a small boggy cwm, where a man-made path and bridge aids walkers. At this stage of the route there are good views of the Glyderau over to the right, and down the Llanberis Pass towards Llyn Peris and Llyn Padarn at the end of the valley. This valley shows the characteristic U-shape caused by the scouring action of the massive glacier that moved down it during the last Ice Age, and, until comparatively recently (geologically speaking), the whole valley was covered with trees. Here, the crags overhead are known as Captain's Bluff and are frequented by rock-climbers. Ahead on the right, across the side of Cwm Beudy Mawr which slopes down

View back towards Siabod

towards the main A4086 road in the Llanberis Pass, the bold outline of Dinas Mot can be seen at the base of the sweep down from Crib Goch's north ridge. It might seem a short cut route to climb up a red gully on the left of the path round about here, but it is deceptive. In fact it leads onto the top of a ridge that ends above Bwlch-y-moch, so any height gained has to be lost by descending once again in the bwlch. This gully has been made by human erosion, so to prevent further damage, it is recommended that walkers stick to the public footpath.

Just as the main path begins to turn up towards Bwlch-y-moch, there is a junction where a somewhat indistinct path bears to the right, and eventually drops into Cwm Glas. The path to Bwlch-y-moch however, rises up the steep, rocky track and now the summit of Crib Goch can be seen in all its glory, directly ahead. After going around a rocky buttress, the path rises steeply through a narrow pass through some rocks and emerges at Bwlch-y-moch, 700 feet above Pen-y-pass. At Bwlch-y-moch itself, there are wonderful views down into Cwm Dyli, with Y Lliwedd on the far side rising above the opposite shore of Llyn Llydaw. Here the path forks; the left branch is the Pig Track whereas the right fork becomes the start of the route up to Crib Goch.

Glaslyn frozen over

The Pig Track from Bwlch-y-moch undulates slightly across the southern flank of Crib Goch and is an easy walk of about two miles with wonderful views of Llyn Llydaw, Y Lliwedd, Glaslyn, and of course, the front face of Snowdon itself. Also, by looking back, on a clear day there are good views of Moel Siabod. There are no real hard inclines on the path until the last slog up to Bwlch Glas, and this last part of the path is best viewed from a cairn high above Glaslyn where it is recommended that a short stay is made on a conspicuous white quartz platform, not only to prepare oneself for the strenuous climb ahead, but also to admire the wonder of the great mountain from one of the best vantage points in the area. Near here can also be found the remains of the old Britannia copper mine and its old workings, but these must not be explored as they are now in a very dangerous condition.

By following the path around under Crib y Ddysgl, the path eventually joins the Miners' Track, at a junction marked by a large striated boulder which can be an important landmark in winter conditions. From here, it continues upwards and great care must be taken to avoid falling into the open shafts of the old copper mines, especially when the ground is covered with snow. Soon the p ath zig-zags up to the last steep scree loose rock section before it eventually reaches Bwlch Glas. It is on the zig-zags that most care has to be taken in all weathers. In the summer, the path is very dry and the going can be hard on the loose earth and shale. In the winter however, this section of the path becomes quite dangerous, requiring the use of crampons and ice-axes as water freezes on the rock ledges of the track making footing treacherous.

In good snow conditions, the whole slope above Glaslyn becomes an alpine ascent-descent, and it is not at all unusual for a cornice to form overhanging the eastern edge of Bwlch Glas which is not only difficult whilst going up the path, but is often treacherous for walkers on the Llanberis Path who can be seen standing on it to look down onto Glaslyn but don't realise it's there! The top of the path is marked by a large upright standing stone, from where the last climb of 300 feet to the summit of Snowdon can be made on a well-marked path.

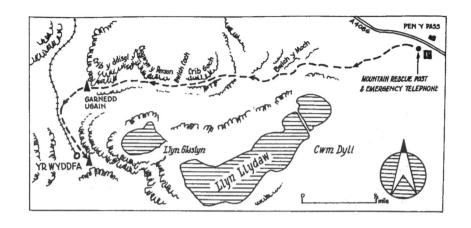

The Crib Goch Route

The route up and over Crib Goch has been described as 'an airy scramble', and indeed it is, requiring every ounce of concentration, and a good deal of nerves for most of its 3 miles to the summit. Vertigo sufferers should not attempt this route! The traverse of this eastern ridge of the Snowdon massif, together with the other eastern ridge – Y Lliwedd, is more commonly known as the Snowdon Horseshoe. It is much easier and safer to climb Crib Goch's eastern edge, than to come down it. Crib Goch, (or the red comb or crest), has it's official summit (3023 ft) at the eastern edge of a very narrow ridge, though the highest point (3026 ft) is actually found at the middle of the crest.

The ascent of Crib Goch proper starts at Bwlch-y-moch, having reached it by following the initial stages of the Pig Track for about a mile. Some people traverse the ridge starting from the Snowdon summit or Crib y Ddysgl end. However it is more advisable to ascend from Bwlch-y-moch, rather than descend to it.

At Bwlch-y-moch, there are wonderful views down into Cwm Dyli, with Y Lliwedd on the far side rising above the opposite shore of Llyn Llydaw. Here the path forks, the left branch remains as a continuation of the Pig Track, whilst the right fork becomes the true start of the route up to Crib Goch. The path from Bwlch-y-moch leads upwards and west, starting over a grassy bank, but

Crib Goch ridge from Bwlch Coch

soon arriving at the base of what is to be a hard climb up a steep rock wall. There is only one really tricky bit, which is almost vertical, but as long as care is taken, it is not insurmountable.

This initial upward path leads to a small rock-wall at the base of the main broken ridge. Some climbers take a direct route up this ridge, but it can be dangerous, especially if there are loose rocks dislodged by climbers up ahead. A safer route is to bear left under the initial rock-wall, and then ascend a ledge that traverses two small rock pitches after which, by bearing right, the main backbone of the ridge can be joined, which rises straight to the summit.

At the summit, there is an excellent view back towards Pen-y-pass and also of the wide north ridge that appears from the right. But it's the very narrow knife-edge ridge directly ahead that leads towards Snowdon, and the Crib Goch proper. The most dangerous part is a 300 feet length which is only about a foot wide, and on a windy day, requires walkers to drop slightly to the left flank, and use the actual crest as a handhold. This knife-edge eventually arrives at the first of the two rock Pinnacles (or *gendarmes*) from where there is a dramatic view of Llyn Glas and Cwm Glas Mawr. It is interesting to look back over the knife-edge from this

The Pinnacles

safer point, and watch the walkers following behind as if each is part of a fragile human chain, all apprehensively waiting to reach the end of this hazard so that they can carry on in relative safety.

The Pinnacles themselves are not too difficult to climb over, although many walkers by-pass the tops by circuiting them on the south (left) flank. The crest of the Pinnacles has one or two sections where you really need at least three appendages on the rock for security, but the rocks are large and quite safe. On the right (north) side of the second pinnacle are four or five very large 'steps' which enable walkers to climb up the top to the other side and then down into the col.

After the Pinnacles, the path arrives at the grassy haven of Bwlch Coch (the red col). Although there are two relatively safe routes off the ridge, one leading north down into Cwm Glas, the other less safe route, south to Cwm Dyli and Llyn Llydaw, these should only be used in an emergency. In fact fences have been erected here to prevent erosion from walkers using such routes off the ridge. There are no other routes off either Crib Goch or Crib y Ddysgl that should be attempted. The main path is the one that leads directly ahead up a slope to the huge perpendicular slabs forming the beginning of Crib y Ddysgl (the crest of the dish).

The highest point on Crib y Ddysgl is Carnedd Ugain (the cairn of twenty) at 3493 feet, and about half a mile up the path to it from Bwlch Coch there is a path to the right that leads off to the Parson's Nose, which is a cliff only for experienced rock-climbers. After the easy ridge from Coch, there is a rock buttress which should be climbed by starting on the left side, and then going up to the right to gain the rock ridge itself. Some walkers have tried to avoid the rock ridge by continuing to the left, but this is a very dangerous route, and there have been many fatalities at this point. In fact this part of the ridge is as difficult in places as the actual Crib Goch section, even though it is less spectacular because there are no sheer drops either side! As with Crib Goch, it is best not to wander off to the left, but instead, stick to the centre up over the crest, where the path eventually leads down to Bwlch Glas.

Bwlch Glas is the cross-roads where three of the main routes on Snowdon meet. From the north the path rises from Llanberis, as does the railway line which now comes into sight. By turning down this path the top of the Snowdon Ranger Path can be reached. From the south the Pig Track rises up the zig-zags and reaches the bwlch at the standing stone, from where there is just a short incline of about half a mile, and about 300 feet of climb up to the summit (fig. 11).

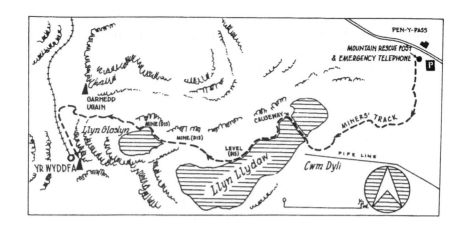

The Miners' Track Route

This is probably the most popular of all the routes up to the summit of Snowdon, or more often just as a leisurely walk to the base of the mountain, at Glaslyn. The path, which starts at the eastern end of the car park at Pen-y-pass, is 3½ miles long, and is quite wide for most of the way, due to its origins as the track by which ore was brought down from the mines around Glaslyn. Furthermore, the track, for most of its length does not have many steep parts, again as this would have caused problems for the miners. In fact, from Pen-y-pass car park to the base of Snowdon at Glaslyn, the path rises just over 750 feet.

As it leaves the car park, the path provides good views to the left of Moel Siabod in the distance, and nearer, the Vale of Gwynant. It then follows the contours around the south-eastern slopes of the Last Nail in the Horseshoe before bearing to the right when the dramatic precipice of Y Lliwedd comes into view. On the left is Cwm Dyli, a valley carved out by a glacier, and now unfortunately the host of the monstrous pipeline that delivers water from Llyn Llydaw to the Cwm Dyli hydro-electric generating station down near Llyn Gwynant. For many years, campaigners have fought for its removal.

At least the beauty of little Llyn Teyrn compensates somewhat for the pipeline, and close to the track on this section the ruins of

Crib Goch ridge from Garnedd Ugain

View back over Crib Goch from Crib y Ddysgl

Miners' Track by Llyn Teryn

Miners' Track and Llyn Llydaw from Y Lliwedd

the old miners' barracks can be seen. Also from here can be seen the conspicuous rocky hill rising out of the valley below. This is consists of dolerite, which cooled after volcanic activity to form hexagonal columns. Now, after glacial action, the flank that faces Snowdon is smooth and rounded, while the opposite flank is steeper and more rugged due to the tearing of the glacial ice.

About half a mile further on, the path reaches the eastern shore of Llyn Llydaw, and it is here that one of the most majestic views of Snowdon can be seen together with a full view of the dramatic dark cliffs of Y Lliwedd on the left, and the Crib Goch ridge on the right. Although on some dull winter days the whole scene can appear foreboding, on a fine sunny summer day the valley at this point exudes an air of absolute tranquillity, and at such a time one can appreciate the peaceful existence that the Celtic tribesmen must have experienced, many years ago. At this point, walkers have a choice of routes to the summit. The main path to the right is the continuation of the Miners' Track, whilst the less well-marked one leading up the grassy slope on the south-west of the lake climbs steadily to the peaks of Y Lliwedd.

The Miners' Track now crosses the famous causeway built to aid the transference of men and ore to and from the mines at Glaslyn and Llydaw. In all but very bad weather the causeway leads walkers to the shore of Llydaw beneath the steep slopes rising to Bwlch-y-moch and the base of Crib Goch. Many years ago after very heavy and continuous rain, the causeway used to become submerged, and a detour around the eastern edge of the lake was necessary .However, since the overflow level has been lowered, such flooding rarely takes place. After the causeway the path meanders around the side of the lake until it arrives at the ruins of the derelict sorting and crushing mills of the Britannia copper mine. Here it is worth stopping to look at the old buildings just to get a feel of the atmosphere that still exists in them, but on no account should they be entered, as they are now in a danger-ous condition. On dull, dreary days, when the mist is swirling around the lake, one can only feel sorry for the men who had to work here in the damp and cold.

From the old mining buildings the path bears right and now steepens quite considerably. The path is actually following the side

The miners' causeway

Ruined mine buildings at the base of Cribyn

Old mine buildings at Llydaw

of the rocky barrier that is the natural dam holding back the waters of Glaslyn. The path then rises towards a natural levelling out at the rim of the basin of the lake near more ruins of mine buildings and it is from here that one of the most impressive views of Snowdon is to be seen. Even on sunny summer days the steep precipices darken the area around this almost circular tarn. In the winter the scene can be really eerie, but at the same time can hold an air of magic especially when the lake is covered with a thick layer of ice. The most dramatic views of Y Lliwedd can be appreciated, and once again one could imagine how demoralising the situation must have been for the poor miners, many years before.

At the part where the Miners' Track levels out near the stream leaving Glaslyn (the source of the river that runs down to the sea at Porthmadog), there is a rocky outcrop rising high to the left. This is the Snowdon Gribin and the summit of this outcrop is at Bwlch-y-Saethau, where the Watkin Path joins the route over to Y Lliwedd. On a summer's day the climb up Gribin is a hard scramble, but beware in the winter as the rocks can be extremely slippery. But it is the winter season that provides the best view of the gullies on Clogwyn y Garnedd which give good snow-climbing when the conditions are right.

The Miners' Track now skirts the north shore of Glaslyn as far as the remains of the barracks of the old copper mines, and it is just after these that the very steep path can be seen (in clear weather!) rising 1300 feet to the saddle of Bwlch Glas. After about 400 feet up the scree climb, the path meets the Pig Track and then both join the zig-zags of what was originally called the Llwybr y mul (the pony track), which was the old name for the Miners' Track. The path is then a hard slog to the standing stone at the Bwlch.

The Watkin Path

This path was named after Sir Edward Watkin who had a chalet near the beginning of the path built so his guests could walk in safety to the top of Snowdon. It was officially opened in 1892 by William Gladstone, who at the age of 83, walked up it to what is now known as the Gladstone Rock. The Watkin Path is probably the hardest of all the paths up Snowdon in terms of climbing height because it starts at the lowest point of all the routes – at the path opposite the car park at Pont Bethania down in Nant Gwynant at just 190 feet above sea level – so provides a climb of 3370 feet (compared with the 2390 feet climb from Pen-y-pass), and all in a distance of just over 3½ miles.

The public right of way (PROW) path begins as a metalled track leading to Hafod y Llan farm, that passes through an oak wood full of large rhododendron bushes, but after going through an iron gate it bears left along a stony track which was originally the old donkey-path constructed by Sir Edward Watkin in 1890. The National Trust has also created a permissive path through the woodland on the left above the PROW which crosses two streams and passes the remains of Sir Edward Watkin's chalet before emerging through a wrought iron gate at a vantage point above Hafod y Llan farm. It is clearly signposted as 'The Watkin Path – path to waterfalls and Snowdon'.

The PROW path widens and curves up above a waterfall and across the remains of the track that was the old slate mine incline. After passing through a second iron (kissing) gate – which is extremely difficult when carrying a rucksack! – the going becomes more rocky. At this point a track goes off down to the right across a stone-slab footbridge, which leads to Gallt y Wenallt, passing many disused mine workings in Cwm Merch. The path climbs quite steeply upwards and narrows, passing old the Hafod-y-Llan mine workings at the side of the Afon Cwm Llan.

Soon, the path levels out and crosses a metal bridge to Plas Cwm Llan where stand the ruins of an old farmhouse, riddled

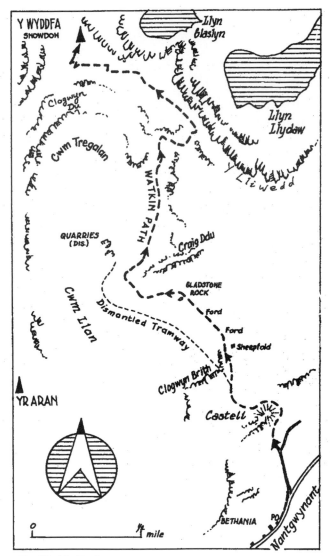

The Watkin Path

with bullet holes from the practice battles of the commandos who trained there in preparation for D-Day. Around the ruin there are also some interesting sheep pens, the sides of which are made from upright large slate slabs. Just before this bridge, a path leads up the slope on the left, and is the start of the path up onto Yr

Hafod-y-Llan ruins by Afon Cwm Llan

Aran. From this spot also, the unimpressive back of Y Lliwedd can be seen, which gives no hint of the sheer precipices on the other side. In fact the whole of Cwm Llan has an air of tranquillity about it, quite unlike the oppressive quality sometimes felt in Cwm Dyli, especially inn the 'bowl', on the other side of the ridge.

The Gladstone Rock is soon reached and a large slate tablet set on a rock commemorates the visit and oration of William Gladstone in 1892. Around 250 yards further on is the Gladstone Slab, the name given to a 100 foot rock-face often used to give beginners their first taste of rock-climbing.

Continuing along the path at no more than a slight incline, the ruins of the dressing sheds and workshops of the South Snowdon

Plas Cwm Llan ruins

slate quarry buildings are reached, which are worth a short visit to sit and ponder on the working conditions of the miners so many years before. On a clear, dry, sunny day in summer, it is worth a detour at this point to go up into Cwm Tregalan to see the old slate quarries. However, such a detour is inadvisable in mist or snow, as there are several very deep pits which can be dangerous. Between the Gladstone Rock and the ruins, the path passes near to a small stream, which can be crossed quite easily. After doing so, there is a path that leads up to the other quarry ruins at Bwlch Cwm Llan, and from here by bearing up to the right (north) the Bwlch Main ridge can be climbed up to the summit of Snowdon.

After the ruins, the Watkin Path narrows and zig-zags sharply up to the right for about 200 feet before bearing left along a slanting incline across the western slopes of Y Lliwedd and facing a new cwm – Cwm Tregalan. On the far side of the cwm the south ridge (Bwlch Main) reaches up to the summit, and on its flanks are the precipices of Clogwyn Du (black precipice). The path continues steadily upwards for about another half mile until at around 2000 feet it turns sharply upwards with still more zig-zagging for another 500 feet or so until arriving at Bwlch Ciliau (the pass of retreat) on the south flanks of Y Lliwedd ridge. From here there is a good view back down Cwm Tregalan where lateral moraines can easily be identified – piles of grass-covered earth and rocks left by the glaciers that carved out the cwm – and also of the peak of Yr Aran with Moel Hebog and the Glaslyn Estuary beyond it, where the waters from Llyn Glaslyn flow into the sea.

Turning left at the bwlch, the path continues almost level along the north side of Cwm Tregalan for about 600 yards until arriving at another bwlch – Bwlch y Saethau (the pass of arrows). Here it is worth going towards the edge overlooking Cwm Dyli from where an astonishing view of the two lakes (Glaslyn and Llydaw) can be seen, against the backdrop of the whole Crib Goch ridge. It is also at this bwlch that the northern ridge of the Snowdon Gribin starts its descent down the rocky arête to the shores of Glaslyn 600 feet below. Although not an extremely difficult descent, more a hard scramble, the route does require a considerable amount of hand and foot work, especially on the steep middle section, which is quite exposed.

From Bwlch y Saethau, the path rises towards the crags and screes below the summit of Snowdon almost 900 feet above, and a direct route over the scree is a very hard climb indeed up the left side of Clogwyn y Garnedd. But is not one that is recommended. Instead, the lower, more accessible path climbs diagonally across the south face of Yr Wyddfa (from bottom right to top left as you look towards the summit) towards the northern edge of Bwlch Main where a standing stone marks the arrival of the path at its junction with the one coming up from Rhyd-ddu. After turning right at the standing stone, the path then climbs steeply over rocky ground finally reaching the summit hotel, 200 feet above.

Sheep folds at Plas Cwm Llan

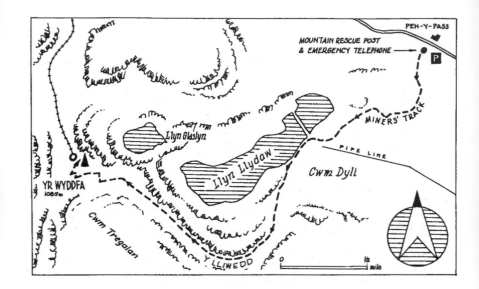

Y Lliwedd Route

The route over Y Lliwedd looks worse than it really is. The over-powering precipices that walkers see when they first catch a glimpse of this part of The Horseshoe are of more concern for climbers than for those wanting to use the ridge as a way of reaching Snowdon's summit. The start of the route proper is from the car park at Pen-y-pass and is the same as that for the Miners' Track until the shores of Llyn Llydaw are reached. Then, instead of bearing right over the causeway, a left turn is made just before the green painted valvehouse shed for the Cwm Dyli pipeline.

After crossing a metal footbridge, the track rises gently at first but then steepens gradually, and care must be taken to follow the left, more distinct track, rather than the indistinct right branch, as the former leads onto the ridge whereas the latter leads to the base of the precipices of Y Lliwedd, which should only be tackled by experienced rock-climbers with the correct equipment.

The path up to the ridge is about three-quarters of a mile and becomes very rough and steep as height is gained. It arrives at the col between Gallt y Wenallt (slope of the white height) at 2032 feet on the left, and Lliwedd Bach on the right, from where there

Y Lliwedd ridge from Lliwedd Bach

is a wonderful view of the ridge ahead. There is a cairn to assist navigation in misty weather, and from this point great care should be taken whilst climbing the crest of the ridge as there is a quite sensational drop on the right for most of the way along the ridge, which requires extreme care in very windy or icy conditions.

The first incline leads to Lliwedd Bach which is of no real stature, but from where there is a good view down to Llyn Gwynant, and eastward over to Moel Siabod. At this point it is important to resist the temptation to follow the 'siren path' up the gully to the left which seems to skirt this part of the climb, and to continue instead up the path which leads to the East Peak of Y Lliwedd. Here the path comes precariously close to what can only be described as 'thin air' as the vertical rock face at this point drops down to Llyn Llydaw over 1,000 feet below, and extreme care should be taken just near the summit, especially in misty or wintry conditions, especially at the point where the path is just inches away from a sheer gully.

From the summit there then follows a slight drop to a small col between the main peaks, and then another rise to what is considered to be the main peak of Y Lliwedd, the West Peak. The path remains very close to the edge so extreme caution is still needed,

Looking back to Bwlch y Saethau from Lliwedd East

The standing stone at Bwlch Main

but it is the West Peak that provides the best vantage point of the Snowdon Horseshoe.

Here, it is worth stopping not only to rest, but also to look both back along the ridge to Moel Siabod to the east; the Glyderau to the north east; the lakes of Glaslyn and Llydaw; Cwm Tregalan and the sea beyond. However it is to view the majesty of the summit of Snowdon directly ahead (providing the weather is favourable!) that must make this one of the most dramatic vantage points on the whole of The Snowdon Horseshoe. Still remembering that it is very close to the precipitous edge, the rocky path now drops down over boulders where extra care must be taken in wet weather, and finally levels out to reach Bwlch y Saethau, where it is joined by the Watkin Path coming up on the left from Cwm Llan.

From the bwlch, the path rises at the steepest angle of its entire length up the 900 feet to the summit. Two routes are available from the bwlch – the one on the right being the most direct but a steep rock climb and is not recommended. The one on the left which takes a more oblique approach (from bottom right to top left as you look at it) is the correct one to take, which eventually joins the Rhyd-ddu Path at the standing stone just above Bwlch Main, before turning right to arrive just below the summit hotel.

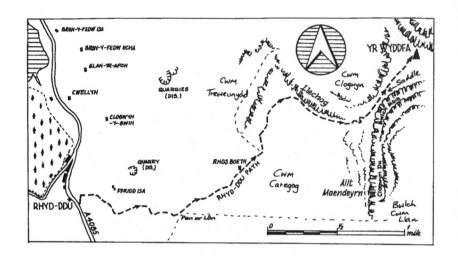

The Rhyd-ddu Path

The Rhyd-ddu path is one of the easiest but probably least used of the main routes to Yr Wyddfa, though during the summer it can get quite busy. The 3¼ mile route provides a mixture of terrain, from boggy grassland to narrow ridge paths and even if it doesn't have the excitement of the precipices of Y Lliwedd or Crib Goch, or the dramatic views of the Pig or Miners' Tracks, nevertheless, it is one of the more scenic routes to the summit. The views both in front as the climb progresses, and looking back towards the Nantlle Ridge over Llyn Cwellyn, are really magnificent.

Until the latest OS Landranger maps were published, this was called the Beddgelert Route, because years ago, walkers used to start the walk at Beddgelert. Now there are in fact two starting points to the Rhyd-ddu Path. One begins at Pitt's Head on the Beddgelert-Caernarfon road and is favoured by walkers without a car as the only parking facilities are the limited ones obtained by permission from Ffridd Uchaf farm, which this path passes. For those with cars, the path beginning from the car park which was once the old South Snowdon station of the Welsh Highland Railway is more convenient.

The Rhyd-ddu Path proper begins by passing through an iron

kissing gate just north of the car park onto a broad track that winds gently eastward uphill. On the left is a small round tower which used to be the powder house for the now disused Ffridd slate quarry. Soon the track divides, the left fork leads down to Ffridd Isaf farm, and the right one climbs gently up past the old waste tip, ruined buildings, and workings of the quarry.

After passing over three stiles, a large rock is seen on which is a faint handwritten notice saying 'Snowdon, first gate on left', and just beyond this point, the path bears to the left where there is another kissing gate. For many years this gate was known as 'the Cogwheel Gate' because it used an old cogwheel as a weight to keep the gate shut, but now there are two iron rods instead. This gate is at the point which is a criss-cross of four paths. Here the Rhyd-ddu Path proper meets the other Beddgelert path coming up from Ffridd Uchaf, and also the path straight-ahead (east-ward) which leads to Cwm Llan, via Bwlch Cwm Llan on the south ridge of Snowdon. This path runs by the ruins of the South Snowdon Quarries, and even passes over the old spoil-heaps to reach the actual bwlch from where, by bearing right down an old slate mound, the walker can head east to join the Watkin Path at Plas Cwm Llan.

The Rhyd-ddu Path to the summit continues through the kissing gate, then dips down over a stream where the ground becomes very boggy in wet weather, before rising again to reach a rocky outcrop from where some superb panoramic views back over Llyn Cwellyn can be appreciated. Soon after passing first through a gap in an old stone wall that runs diagonally across the path, and then over a stile in a wall at right angles to the path, a grassy terrace is reached near the ruins of a small hut. This hut was, long ago, the half-way house where an old lady and her son made refreshments for walkers.

The grassy terrace is called Mur-y-muriau (enclosure of enclosures), and traditionally the site of a very holy place used by the druids. After passing through a further gate in a stone wall at about 2000 feet, the ground steepens considerably to the main shoulder of Llechog. At this point, on a clear day, the views are really splendid. Up on the skyline, the outline of the Snowdon summit buildings can be seen, and down in the valley on the left

Looking back towards Mynydd Drws-y-Coed and Rhyd Du village

Llyn Nadroedd

(north) is Cwm Clogwyn with its five small lakes. On the right is Cwm Caregog.

Cwm Clogwyn (the hollow of the precipice) gets its name from the sheer wall of shale and loose rocks that falls 1800 feet from the summit just beneath the hotel. This rock wall, together with the rock-face of Llechog, give the cwm a distinct gloom, added to which it is shaded from the sun for most of the time. The cwm has two parts to it, the inner cwm, nearest to Llechog contains the three small lakes – Llyn Glas, Llyn Coch, and Llyn Nadroedd (the lake of serpents) which is the most picturesque. At the north-west end of this inner cwm, the land drops steeply to the outer part of the cwm where another small lake – Llyn Treweunydd, and the largest of the five – Llyn Ffynnon-y-gwas (the man-servant's well) are found, the latter being a reservoir. Entry to Cwm Clogwyn is normally made from the Snowdon Ranger Path, though it can be reached from the Rhyd-ddu Path by bearing left at the second gate mentioned earlier, and crossing the grassy mountainside in a northerly direction just below the rocks that are the start of the Llechog ridge.

Cwm Caregog (the stony hollow) is one of the least visited parts of Snowdon. This is probably because of all the cwms on Snowdon, this one has no obvious points of interest – no lakes, no waterfalls, no real climbing precipices, in fact, little stunning scenery at all. What it has got however, is wonderful peace and serenity, which to me is all important, as there are few parts of Snowdon where such tranquillity remains. There is no recognised path through this cwm, but from the Rhyd-ddu Path at the grassy terrace of Mur-y-muriau, turn due east at the stone wall on the 1600 feet contour, and head for the small gap in the south ridge on the skyline, called Allt or Bwlch Maenderyn (col of the bird stone). From here by turning left (north) the Bwlch Main ridge can be climbed to the summit.

The Rhyd-ddu path now heads up over Llechog and although it is steep it is relatively safe for most of the way. The path first crosses another stream and ascends steeply to another wall. This section of the path is well marked by cairns but is very rough and uneven and care is needed in wet weather or wintry conditions. After crossing through a gap in the wall, the path comes onto the

Llyn Coch and Llyn Glas in Cwm Clogwyn

shoulder of the Llechog ridge, and from here there are excellent views across Cwm Clogwyn down towards Llanberis and also back over Llyn Cwellyn. Continuing up to the right, the path climbs the Llechog ridge itself, over bleak and windswept terrain. This side of the Snowdon massif is very exposed to the prevailing winds, particularly in the winter, and the landscape reflects this, dominated by frost-shattered rocks and very little vegetation.

After a short distance the same wall is reached further up the ridge, and after passing through it once more, and turning sharp left, the path continues on the level for a while but soon begins to climb quite steeply, and in snow and ice conditions, this part of the route can also be quite treacherous.

Here the path has also become very badly eroded, and barrier fences have been erected to divert walkers on to a more stable zig-zag route, after which the path gets very close to the steep scree slopes down into Cwm Clogwyn. Soon it reaches the beginning of Bwlch Main, known as 'the Saddle'. From here there are marvellous views down into Cwm Tregalan with the Watkin Path and Y Lliwedd on the right; and Cwm Clogwyn and the Snowdon Ranger Path on the left; and back down Bwlch Main over to Yr Aran. The 'Saddle' is also the point where the path from the South Ridge comes down from the right to join the Rhyd-ddu Path.

The path continues up the quite narrow col of Bwlch Main (the slender passage) which was originally called Clawdd Coch (the red dyke), and which is extremely exposed to the wind from both sides. Although the path is perfectly safe, great care has to be maintained, especially in wintry conditions, as there are steep drops on each side. Soon the path of Bwlch Main reaches a much broader piece of land, and it is then only 500 feet or so of a rocky scramble up to the summit. On the right is a large standing stone which marks the best starting point of the path down to Bwlch y Saethau, and eventually either over Y Lliwedd or down the Watkin Path.

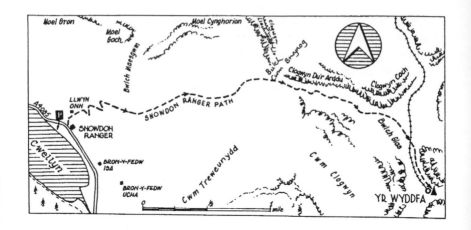

The Snowdon Ranger Path

Like the Llanberis Path route, being just over 3½ miles, this one provides an easy and pleasant ascent, with the one major difference – unlike the former, this path does not have many sheer drops near it, although it does get close to the top edge of Clogwyn Du'r Arddu at one point! This is probably the oldest route to the summit and is named after John Morton, the first guide, who opened the Snowdon Ranger Inn, the building on the A487 beside Llyn Cwellyn which is now a youth hostel bearing the same name. In fact in George Borrow's *Wild Wales* it's reported that whilst the author was wandering nearby, a young man informed him:

> A ranger means a guide, sir, my father-in-law is generally termed the Snowdon Ranger because he is a tip-top guide and has named the house after himself.

In fact the name ranger stems from the time of Elizabeth I, when Snowdonia was a Royal Forest, and Robert Dudley, Earl of Leicester, held the position of Ranger of Snowdon, whereupon guides of the eighteenth century took it upon themselves to adopt the title too.

The path itself starts at a stile to the left of the hostel where, after crossing the old track of the Welsh Highland Railway, it passes Llwyn Onn farm further up the hillside before zig-zagging across the pastures above it, to a gate in a stone wall. Just before the wall, a smaller path is to be found branching up to the left, which leads to Bwlch Maesgwm between Foel Goch and Moel Cynghorion, and eventually reaches Llanberi s. By looking back at this point, a marvellous view over Llyn Cwellyn is gained with Mynydd Mawr rising above it, and the Nantlle Ridge and Moel Hebog in the distance behind.

After passing through the gate, the land levels out considerably, and crosses over marshy ground which although is quite easy to follow, can become very boggy after rain. Over to the right, is Cwm Clogwyn in all its tranquillity, and between the path and a small nameless reservoir-lake is Maen Bras, the large boulder which was transported to its current position by glacier. From here can also be seen the waste tips of the Glanrafon Slate Quarry in the valley below. After crossing a stream and continuing through another gate, the path rises up a slight gradient and in front is Bwlch Cwm Brwynog in between the two ridges – Clogwyn Du'r Arddu on the right, leading up to Snowdon, and Clogwyn Llechwedd Llo, that leads up to Moel Cynghorion. Just as the path approaches the bwlch, it bears to the right from where a good view of Llyn Ffynnon-y-gwas is obtained with the Llechog ridge in the distance.

The path then climbs behind the lake almost to the bwlch, before curving to the east where it begins the steep zig-zags up onto the ridge above Clogwyn Du'r Arddu. At this point it is worth walking directly up to the bwlch to appreciate the views not only down into Cwm Brwynog with the Llanberis Path over to the right, but also the views behind back over to Moel Hebog, Moel Lefn, Mynydd Drws-y-coed and Y Garn, with the Beddgelert Forest covering their lower slopes.

Just below the bwlch in Cwm Brwynog, the Afon Arddu rises, and then flows down the cwm into Llanberis. A narrow path leads eastwards from the bwlch across the steep slopes at the head of the cwm, around under the crags, eventually passing through a pile of boulders to reach Llyn Du'r Arddu. Behind the lake rises the almost vertical Clogwyn rock-face, known affectionately as

Walkers on the Snowdon Ranger Path on Clogwyn Du'r Arddu

'Cloggy' to most rock climbers. This is a most impressive precipice, the true scale of which can be best appreciated if there happen to be climbers on it, when their almost ant-sized bodies are just to be seen. The most usual translation of Clogwyn Du'r Arddu is the black cliff of the black height, which really sums up the dark and eerie scene characteristic of this formidable precipice. Furthermore, because of its position under the rockface, when approached from the north – the usual approach – Llyn Du'r Arddu rarely looks any colour other than black, which enhances the sombreness of the place.

Although the precipice is only 500 feet high, less than Y Lliwedd for example, climbers have a strong affinity with it, perhaps because it was on this rock-face in 1799 that the first rock-climb in Wales was made by the Rev. Peter Williams, Rector of Llanrug and Llanberis, accompanied by the famous Rev. Bingley. Whilst collecting plant specimens at the base of the East Buttress they decided to see if they could reach some further up the rock-face, and then thought they might as well carry on up to the top! It wasn't until more than a hundred years later, that P.S. Thompson could claim to be the first true rock-climber to ascend the now famous deep Chimney on the Far West Buttress.

Clogwyn Station from Clogwyn Du'r Arddu

On the plateau behind the lake one can often see tents pitched and I'm sure this area provides a most dramatic camp site. A route can be made up to the Llanberis Path from there by taking the old miners path to the junction with the Llanberis Path at the base of the Allt Moses section. The Snowdon Ranger Path proper continues up the crest of the ridge immediately above the Clogwyn precipice, and after about a half-mile of gentle rise, joins the Llanberis Path at a point marked by a standing stone just near Bwlch Glas, from where by turning right, the summit can be attained.

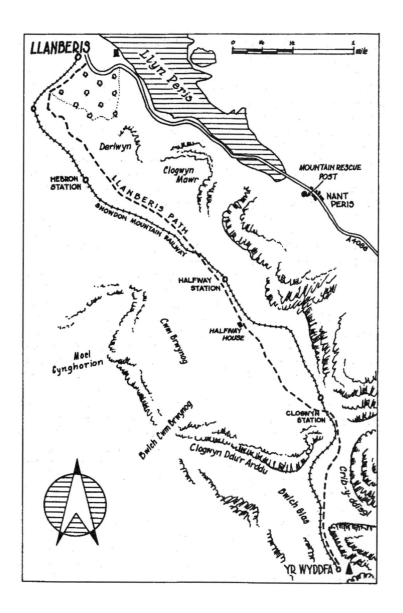

The Llanberis Path

This is the longest but easiest route to the summit, and consequently the most popular and generally the busiest. It is a walk of about five miles from base to summit along the turfy rather than rocky north-west ridge and is well graded, broad, and easy under foot. For most of its length it travels close to the Snowdon Mountain Railway, and in fact for the last 500 yds of ascent the two tracks are only inches apart.

The walk begins on the road opposite the Royal Victoria Hotel in Llanberis, and soon becomes very steep for about a quarter of a mile past the small wood, Coed Victoria. The tarmac road then continues up a steep gradient past a cottage, after which the path to the summit becomes a stoney track which bears left up towards the unfenced mountainside. At this stage, help is given in the form of a notice-board style map of the area and the route of the path, so adequate bearings can be taken whilst catching breath from the hard initial climb. Whilst doing so, it is also well worth surveying the scene all around. Behind are the slate quarries of Dinorwig, the slopes of which rise up to the summit of Elidir Fawr. To the right the Moel Eilio range stands gloriously: Moel Eilio, Foel Gron, Foel Goch, and finally straight ahead, Moel Cynghorion with Bwlch Cwm Brwynog between it and Clogwyn Du'r Arddu.

After going through a gate, the path continues upwards, then bears right over rocky ground which after a wet spell can be quite slippery. After about a mile, the it passes under the railway line which then rises up to the left of the path onto the Llechog ridge (not to be confused with the other Llechog ridge on the Rhyd-ddu Path). A further half-mile from this bridge Halfway House is reached – a welcome sight (and site) on both a hot or a wet summer's day. Here, the owners open daily from May to September, to serve light refreshments. D u ring the winter months, the hut is boarded up and locked, so this is no refuge when closed.

The hardest part of the route now begins. The path steepens, gradually at first, but then quite severely. As it bears to the left, the

The view up Cwm Brwynog

dark face of Clogwyn Du'r Arddu rises above Llyn Du'r Arddu. This rock face provides some of the best climbing rock in Wales, but is strictly for the experienced. At this point there is a cairn marking a divergence of the path. The right fork continues on a more or less level contour, and this was the old miners' track to the now disused copper mines on the slopes of Clogwyn Coch, to the left of Clogwyn Du'r Arddu, but is now mainly used by climbers to reach these world famous cliffs.

The main Llanberis Path is the one that climbs steeply up to the left at which point it is locally known as 'Allt Moses' or 'Moses Hill', and at 2600 feet it again passes under the railway track just up above Clogwyn Station which is on the high bank to the left of the path. Great care must be taken at this point, especially in the winter, because after emerging from under the railway bridge, the

The Snowdon train approaching Halfway Halt

Halfway House

path takes a sharp right-handed turn up an exposed gradient. More importantly, although there is a spectacular view over the Llanberis Pass below, and with the Glyderau on the skyline, there is also a considerable and awesome drop down into Cwm Hetiau, which can be quite unnerving to the uninitiated. There is a possible, but very tricky, descent down into Cwm Glas Mawr from the path about a quarter of a mile up the incline, at a point just where the path starts climbing steeply above the railway line. However, this route should certainly not be attempted in misty conditions.

Continuing onto the Llanberis route up to the summit, the path now rises up an incline, which is mainly loose rock over grass, under the dome of Crib y Ddysgl and this section can be quite treacherous in the winter. In fact the National Park Authority have placed warning notices near this section. The path eventually crosses the top of the incline above the railway line which is now below to the right. However, do not be tempted to walk up the railway track as not only is it strictly prohibited by the Railway Company, it is also dangerously exposed in misty and wintry conditions.

Soon the standing stone at Bwlch Glas is gained, and here there is another spectacular view down into Cwm Dyli, and over the two lakes – Glaslyn and Llyn Llydaw. Again, care should be taken at this point, especially in mist, as on the left there is quite a considerable drop down onto the Pig Track. In the winter, extreme care must be taken here as cornices often form, which can be very dangerous. Furthemore, there is usually a strong wind at this Bwlch all year round, also calling for extra care to be taken.

After dropping down over a small wall to the right, the path follows the railway line the last few hundred yards up to the summit. Although this looks, and is, an easy walk in the summer, in the winter this part of the path is often under many feet of snow which blows and drifts onto this exposed section, and often makes further progress impossible. Soon the restaurant comes into view, and eventually, by climbing up the rocks to the left, the summit cairn is reached.

For those who want one of the best experiences of their lives, a walk up the Llanberis Path overnight during the summer months when there is a clear sky and a full moon to provide all the light you'll need, is highly recommended, and a walk you'll never forget. It's best to plan to reach the summit about an hour before sunrise, and watch the sky turn all shades of pink, purple, orange red, and yellow as the sun comes up from behind the direction of Moel Siabod.

Llyn Du'r Arddu and Clogwyn

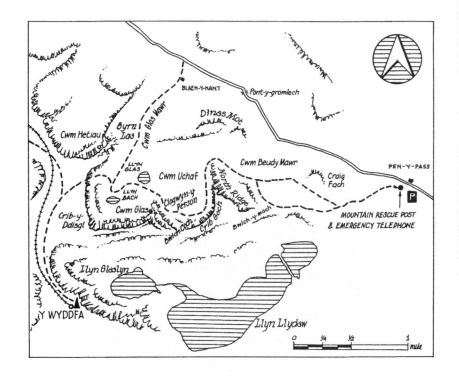

The Cwm Glas Routes

These routes are two of the least used and for that reason are often the nicest because of their tranquillity. There are two starts – one from Pen-y-pass which gives a walk of about 3 miles, the other from the Llanberis Pass which is about 2 miles. Both make use of the ridges that run from the Crib Goch route down towards the Llanberis Pass, and the other common feature is both routes can end up at Llyn Glas before the steep climb onto the Crib Goch ridge.

From Pen-y-pass, the first route starts in the same way as the Pig Track but just as the path turns left to climb up to Bwlch-y-moch, there is a rather indistinct path, the start of which is marked by a small cairn that drops down to the right, contouring WNW on a grassy terrace below. Ahead is the wide area of rock, turf, and

Llyn Glas and Clogwyn y Person

bog – Cwm Beudy Mawr (the hollow of the big cow-house), whilst high up to the left is the north ridge onto Crib Goch. The path dips and rises across the rather rocky mountainside at about the 1400 feet contour, and is well cairned. From here it is best to aim for a notch in the north ridge well above Dinas Mot. If you drop down onto Dinas Mot itself, there is a very steep and awkward climb back up into Cwm Uchaf, involving crossing a waterfall which could be very dangerous in full flow. By turning left up the north ridge, with care, a rocky scramble can be made to join the start of the Crib Goch Route.

From the north ridge the path is now a partially cairned one and goes around a corner into Cwm Uchaf where up on the left are tremendous views of Clogwyn y Person, and the Pinnacles of

The path into Cwm Glas from the Llanberis Pass

Crib Goch. Down to the right is Cwm Glas Mawr, dropping towards the Llanberis Pass. Ahead lies Llyn Glas – probably one of the most beautifully situated tarns in Wales. After turning the corner into Cwm Uchaf, it is advisable not to follow the cairns downwards, but rather to keep on an upwards route above the lip of the cwm until a line of bigger cairns is reached at which point also the red scree leading up to Bwlch Coch can be seen above. There is now a well-defined path that those with some experience of scrambling can attempt to reach the Crib Goch ridge, but this route is not advisable for beginners.

The large cairns lead on to Llyn Glas and now, looking up to the left, the superb arête can be seen stretching from Clogwyn y Ddysgl and ending in the famous Parson's Nose, a popular climbing route for experienced rock-climbers, but not a route up for the average walker. To reach the ridge from here, the gully must be found on the west side behind the Nose, by which, with some hard scrambling, the Crib y Ddysgl ridge can be attained.

Going around the path at the base of Clogwyn y Person, a smaller lake is reached (Llyn Bach), from where the full length of Cwm Glas can be seen falling below into Cwm Glas Mawr, and eventually down to the Llanberis Pass. Ahead is the Llanberis

Steep section in Cwm Glas Mawr

ridge on which the Snowdon Railway runs, and it is this that should be aimed for as the remainder of the route to the summit. Looking west from Llyn Bach, a steep grassy and rocky bank rises almost vertically up to the skyline between the rocks flanking a scree gully on the left, and a grey buttress on the right. By finding two rocky steps in the middle of the bank, a slight scramble leads to an easier walk in an upward direction to the right, eventually arriving on the Llanberis ridge just above Clogwyn Station from where the main Llanberis Path route can be joined to the summit.

The second, alternative way of reaching Cwm Glas is from the Llanberis Pass, but this is a much harder route involving a climb of almost 2,000 feet over a very short distance. However, the effort is worth it if only for the atmosphere of being enclosed in the cwm, with the oppressive but stunning Crib Goch ridge demonstrably on the skyline. The start of this route is the small bridge over the Afon Nant Peris near Blaen-y-nant. After crossing this bridge and going over the stile, another small bridge of railway sleepers is reached, at which point a sharp turn to the left should be made to walk up the right bank of the stream. By following the rather indistinct path a wall is reached, and after passing through a gap in it, a more distinct path is found, leading upward into Cwm Glas Mawr.

Head for a gap between Craig y Rhaeadr (waterfall crag) on the left and the rock face of Gyrn Las (the green horn) on the right. This is another popular rock-climbing area, on which can be found many modern classic climbs. The way up from here is either directly but steeply up the left side of the cascading stream, or by the slightly easier route through a shallow gully further over to the left. However both routes involve very hard work as the paths are of loose rock and in some places are almost vertical. By crossing two further streams and scrambling up a relatively steep bank Llyn Glas is reached, from where the routes onto either the Crib Goch, or Llanberis ridges can be found as previously described.

In reverse, this route is also an alternative one back to Pen-y-pass by descending the steep rock and scree path from Cwm Glas, to Blaen-y-nant, and then walking up the Llanberis Pass (or catching a Sherpa bus!).

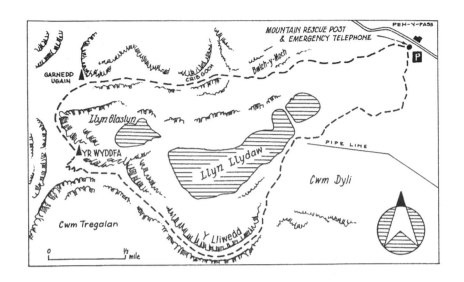

The Snowdon Horseshoe

This is one of the most superb ridge walks in Britain, if not in Europe. As its name suggests, it is U-shaped on a map, although in practice it is circular, both starting and ending at Pen-y-pass. It is 7½ miles in length, and in good weather should take an average fit person about six hours to complete. In winter conditions, this walk is strictly for the very experienced mountaineer.

It can be done in either direction, most people do it anti-clockwise, by starting at Pen-y-pass, going first to Bwlch-y-moch, up over the Crib Goch ridge to the summit (see pages 81-84). Then down to Bwlch y Saethau, over the two peaks of Y Lliwedd, down to the causeway of Llyn Llydaw, and finally walking the Miners' Track back to Pen-y-pass (see pages 85-91, but in reverse).

Purists feel they ought to start the walk by taking in the Horns just above the start of the Miners' Track, but not only does this mean that it is not so direct a route to Bwlch-y-moch, but for conservation reasons, National Park wardens prefer walkers not to walk over this area. One thing is certain, if the weather is good, and the clouds are high, you're sure of one of the best walks of your life, so don't forget your camera!

Visitors to Snowdon

Amongst the hills and mountains of Wales the area around Snowdon has attracted the most visitors and also the many writers, as the Snowdon massif itself is of great significance to Welsh people. It is a traditional hub of their universe, perhaps mainly because it was to such a place that popular leaders such as Owain Glyndwr retreated to revitalise their men for future battles, safe in the knowledge that their enemies often hesitated before following them to such barren and wild parts.

When walking on Snowdon, I often wonder about the people who have walked the same paths during the centuries before me. It is so easy to forget that the climbing of mountains by travellers and visitors is a modern development. As a sport or pastime, mountaineering hardly existed in this country until it became popular in the Alps, less than a century ago. The early travellers who have left records of their adventures on Snowdon often climbed it not so much for the pleasure of the sport, but rather in pursuit of different goals, whether as botanists, geologists, cartographers or antiquarians. To them, Snowdonia was an unknown area to be approached with misgiving, to be traversed with dread, and to be subsequently described in their own scientific languages. During the seventeenth and most of the eighteenth centuries there was good reason for this apprehension.

Exploration on mountains like Snowdon had not begun in any serious manner. The guide books which we now take for granted did not exist. The maps of the time gave no indication of the true nature of the country, unlike the accurate information provided by Ordnance Survey publications. Furthermore, the absence of any general knowledge of the massif required the employment of local men as both guides and interpreters, as few of the inhabitants spoke English, and still fewer travellers understood Welsh.

Of the visitors who came to Snowdon, the earliest recorded was Giraldus Cambrensis, in 1188. In the centuries that followed, many other famous and ordinary travellers visited the massif, some to climb it, others merely to observe its presence from below. We know that John Leland arrived there in 1536, and was followed in 1586 by William Camden, both of whom left quite descriptive accounts of their visits. But it was not until 1639 that the first actual ascent to the summit was recorded, by the botanist Thomas Johnson, who together with a boy guide, climbed "...a way which is narrow and rather precipitous, rough with sharp crags on both sides which strike the utmost horrors into those who are ascending". Various experts have speculated which route he was describing, but my theory is that it was either via Bwlch Main, or Crib Goch – though we'll never really know.

Johnson was followed by Halley (of the comet), Defoe, and eventually in 1774 by Dr Johnson, the first true tourist: a visitor who came to Snowdon for leisure purposes rather than to study. In fact, between 1790 and 1800, eleven books were published detailing tours in north Wales. The first, by Thomas Champion, was the *Observation of a Tour of Snowdon* in 1735. There followed Lord Lyttleton in 1755 who unfortunately (somewhat like many of today's tourists) was denied the view from the summit because "...Snowdon was wrapt in cloud from top to bottom".

Joseph Craddock's *Letters from Snowdon* published in 1770 was followed by probably the most famous of all travellers to North Wales – Thomas Pennant, whose *Tour of Wales*, published in 1781 became the accepted authority on Snowdonia. In 1796, Arthur Aikin published *Journal of a Tour through North Wales and Parts of Shropshire*, but unfortunately he too arrived at Snowdon on a miserable day when "the wind was high and cold so piercing as to make us take shelter" – an experience I'm sure we've all felt before! In 1797, The Rev. Richard Warner wrote about *A Walk Through Wales* but at least his journey was more worthwhile "our toil at first seemed ill repaid. Cloud still covered the top and we remained involved in mist which produced a most intense cold.... The mist gradually sailed away and left us to contemplate for a moment at a wide and unclouded prospect of mountains and valleys, cities, lakes and oceans." Another cleric – the Rev. W. Bingley followed Warner, and published *A Tour Round North Wales*. It is thought that he was one of the first to scale the danger-ous cliffs of Clogwyn Du'r Arddu, now a favourite haunt of rock-climbers. As Bingley was nearing the end of his journey, another traveller, John Evans, was starting his.

Amazingly, Evans was also a cleric, which makes one wonder whether there was some divine force drawing so many religious people to this part of Wales, or was it that the clerics of those days had more leisure-time than other professions? (In future, I will check for clerical collars on my walks to the summit!) Evans tried to reach the summit many times but the weather continuously prevented him. In fact he never climbed Snowdon. Instead, he visited the surrounding areas, the details of which were eventually published in a series of books, generally titled *The Beauties of England and Wales*.

The last of the major eighteenth century visitors to this great mountain was W. Hutton, whose resulting book was *Remarks upon North Wales*. Hutton was another who tried, unsuccessfully, many times to climb to the summit of Snowdon but was prevented by low cloud and generally bad weather. Finally, on September 6th, 1799, Hutton, his servant, and a guide reached the summit on a gloriously hot day, allowing him to add the details of his view into his publication. More important though was the fact that, as he said "It was the hardest labour of my whole life and perhaps I am the only man who ever took a wanton trip to the summit of Snowdon at the age of 76."

After Hutton, the numbers of visitors dramatically increased, and in general they were younger and less professional than those of the late eighteenth century. The early nineteenth century brought with it not only more people, but also more changes in the whole surrounding area as more roads were opened up. Tourism had reached Snowdon, and with it the need for places for the tourists to stay, and guides to help them achieve their objectives and aspirations!

Although there have been a number of hotels catering for tourists to Snowdonia, there has probably been only one that has catered for those visitors that have had a true love of Snowdon itself. For almost two hundred years, a refuge has stood on the same spot, even though in the very early days it was just a cottage owned by a man called John Roberts, who supplied food and beer to weary travellers. Nowadays it is known as the P.Y.G. – the

Penygwryd Hotel, and is the hub of most walking and climbing activities in the area.

For many years it was run by that famous climber and mountain rescue man Chris Briggs and his wife Jo, and during that time, many walkers and climbers, both ordinary and famous have been grateful for the comfort and good food and drink that have made their visit to Snowdon all the more memorable. Many of them have also been allowed to record their thought and feelings in the now famous 'locked' visitors book, which I had the honour of being able to read on one of my visits, and some have even left their mark in more artistic ways in sketch and cartoon form.

The fact that the 1953 Everest expedition used the hotel whilst training in Snowdonia has also helped to make it a famous haunt of climbers, and still today, relics of the team's equipment, together with other artifacts relating to that epic time, can be seen dotted around the various rooms and bars. It is also no mere coincidence that one of the most popular tracks to the summit is thought to have been named after the hotel – the Pig Track. Nowadays the P.Y.G. is superbly looked after by Chris's daughter Jane, and her husband Brian, and it is worth a visit even if only to have a drink in the bar and savour the atmosphere.

With the increase in tourism, not only did hotels necessary, but also mountain guides

"You know the way to Snowdon?"
"I ought to, sir, I've been trying it nigh forty years."
"You seem old. I suppose you don't go often now?"
"No. Never more than twice a day."

Thus went a conversation in 1880, between a visitor and a local guide at what was then probably the other hotel most used by walkers and climbers – the Royal Hotel at Capel Curig (now Plas y Brenin, the National Sports Activity Centre). Today, I doubt whether anyone in the locality of Snowdon climbs it as regularly, or as a guide as in the old meaning of the word (the exception being the National Park wardens).

Until well into the twentieth century, it was considered foolish to climb the mountain without a recognised guide, unless you were a highly qualified mountaineer, as the risks were thought to be very considerable. Such caution was naturally heavily promoted by the guides, and ensured a lucrative income.

However, even if it paid relatively well, it was not easy work. A guide was expected not only to know the best and usually easiest route, but also to carry any picnic, and lead the horse that the visitors might have wanted to ride on. But though it was hard work, it was regarded as a better occupation than that of a peasant farmer or worse still, a copper miner.

Originally the guides were local men, employed to take travellers from village to village across the untracked mountain. In the 1800s, the paths that tourists and walkers tread today weren't as eroded or as clear, and it is hard to imagine finding your way up the Snowdon Ranger route with no path or a book like this to follow! It has also to be remembered that although the guides were best known for their trips up Snowdon, they also helped visitors to cross the Glyderau and the Carneddau too, well into the nineteenth century. Over the years certain guides became better known than others, either for their individual assets such as charm, companionship, knowledge, care, or overall reputation. Some of the best known of the eighteenth century Snowdon guides were Hugh Shone, who was the guide that Pennant preferred; William Lloyd, a schoolmaster in Beddgelert who normally only climbed in school holidays; John Closs, and the parish clerk (known as the Llanberis Clerk) both from Llanberis; Evan Jones, a waiter at the Royal Hotel, Capel Curig, and Robert Hughes who took over from him; and Henry Owen from the Penygwryd Hotel.

As proof of Henry Owen's reputation, his epitaph on a tablet in Beddgelert church states:

> To the memory of Henry Owen.
> For 44 years landlord of the Inn at Pen-y-Gwryd
> and guide to Snowdon.
> In business, Upright and Courteous.
> In Service, Strong and Patient.
> In Friendship, Simple and Sincere.
> This tribute is erected by old friends who Knew
> and Honoured Him.
>
> Born April 2 1822   Died May 5 1891

Miner's track by Llyn Teyrn

Zig Zags above Glaslyn

View down Llanberis Pass from Pyg Track

Old mine buildings at Llydaw

Start of climb up Crib Goch

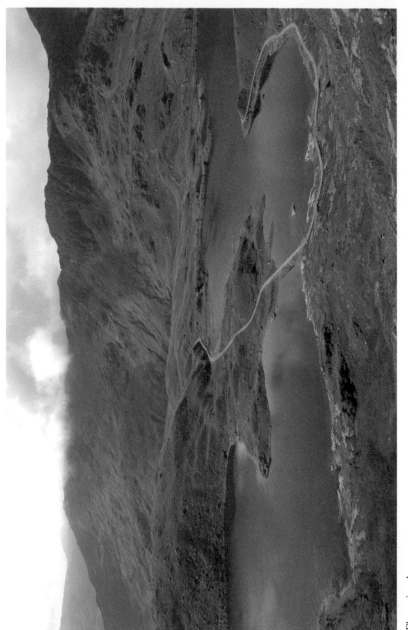

The miner's causeway

Y Lliwedd Ridge from the Pyg Track

Snowdon rising from Glas Llyn

These were some of the more well-known guides, but there were many more equally qualified guides that remain unknown or unrecognised. Throughout the nineteenth century these others were ordinary local villagers who happened to know their way up Snowdon, including a young boy – Edward Lias – who was a mere thirteen year old, and Tom Jones of Beddgelert who was in his seventies when he retired. Some of the guides became well known and respected, but there were also bad guides who were often unfit, unsure, ill-informed, got lost in mist, and were generally un-cooperative. Fortunately they were in the minority, but they must have occasionally given the trade a bad name. Most regular guides would have climbed Snowdon hundreds or even thousands of times in their lifetime, and because they often carried a 'visitors' book' in which they got their visitors to write glowing testimonials that they could show other potential hirers, these books held a considerable amount of information that now enables us to know more about the guides and their work.

For instance, in Tom Jones' book we learn that one day he took only 1 hour 35 minutes to reach the summit, and just 1 hour 8 minutes to return. We also find that between May and November he climbed the mountain thirty-five times. This was not a great deal though, as other guides' books tell of them making over 3,000 journeys in the course of their working life. Similarly, in the visitors' book from the Royal Hotel in Capel Curig, we read that when he was in his sixties, Robert Hughes, over three consecutive days, climbed Snowdon via the Pig Track and descended via Yr Aran on day one; completed the Snowdon Horseshoe in reverse (by ascending over Y Lliwedd and descending down Crib Goch) on day two; and on the third day ascended the Gribbin ridge between Y Lliwedd and Snowdon and descended via Carnedd Ugain and Cwm Glas. This would be tiring work for even the fittest climbers today!

From early in the nineteenth century, the majority of the guides worked closely with the various hotels in the area around Snowdon. In practice, the guides depended on the hotels for the use of their horses, and also for the introductions to the visitors. The hotels also paid the guides, and compared with nowadays, the costs to the visitors were quite high. The average price for a day was ten shillings, so inevitably it was mainly the upper classes that used the service. As the guides would often take parties of four to six people, this tourist industry was quite lucrative.

As some of the older men retired, younger men and even boys took over. The problem was that in many cases they lacked the experience of the older ones, and in some cases their stamina. What they had, however, was enthusiasm, and although this was an admirable quality when kept under control, at one stage in Llanberis, there were so many guides touting for business, often at ridiculously low rates, that a number of them were prosecuted.

Among the most entrepreneurial guides was J.P. Hamer, who worked from Caernarfon. He was an estate agent, coach proprietor, driver and, above all 'THE Guide to Snowdon' – taking customers up Hamer's Route "...which is not only the best route on Snowdon but the only one which will guarantee a view at the top however misty it is for other routes". I'm sure that if Hamer was alive today he'd be a millionaire if he could guarantee such a walk up to Snowdon, or perhaps the general weather conditions have changed dramatically over the last hundred years!

Hamer also was his own publicist, promoting his tours in a booklet entitled *Hamer's Practical Steamboat Railway and Road Guide*, in which he offered a complete service up Snowdon from Snowdon Ranger by Hamer's Route, or a coach trip around Snowdon with stops at all the required sight-seeing places. The best feature of his services was their all-in packages, starting and finishing at Caernarfon, and including tea.

Another guide who made a name for himself was William Morris from Nant Peris. He was a tenant on a farm situated on a path that provided a short-cut up to the Llanberis Path, avoiding a two mile walk via the village of Llanberis itself. He became concerned about the number of people, often escorted by guides, that walked over his land so he put a lock on the gate to the path. But then he realised that the path was actually an asset, so he came to an agreement with his landlord (the Assheton-Smith Estate) that for an agreed payment, he could charge a fee for walkers to pass over his land, and to do this he set himself up as a guide, the charge for use of the short-cut then being included in his rate.

The major problem visitors found in hiring a guide, was the language barrier. In the eighteenth century, places like Llanberis and Capel Curig were tiny mountain villages and, inevitably, all the villagers spoke only in Welsh. Some of the older guides were quick to learn that if they knew a few basic phrases in English, even if they were merely commands and questions relating to the route and the views, then they had a better chance of being offered work from the hotels than if they knew no English. The younger guides somehow found it easier to learn English!

It is interesting also to ponder on the fact that in those early days of mountaineering, the guides did not have the luxury of Goretex and Vibram, and more often than not climbed in their everyday clothes. One guide, in the late nineteenth century, when asked by one of his customers what clothes should be worn for the trip, answered:

> Roll up your trousers above the knee as there is great ease-ment in stepping high. Pedestrians generally make mistakes regarding their kit, they either burden themselves with too great a weight or do not provide sufficient for health and comfort. Do not take less than an entire change of every-thing. Carry no knapsack but in lieu thereof a simple stout canvas or mackintosh pouch with a turnover, slung over the shoulder with a strap of webbing an inch and a half wide with a buckle, similar in design to a game bag but not so deep. This with an umbrella of the best silk and a stout walking stem with a crutch handle, a strong ferrule and short spike. The pouch is recommended in preference to coat pocket because the weight of contents can be varied in position and does not come into contact with motion of limbs. Knickerbockers are the best wear for nether limbs because they do not confine limbs nor, when wet, hang heavily against the legs. Thick woollen, not worsted, stockings should be worn with leggings, if required, of same material as knickerbockers because, if saturated in peat and mud, and sand, can be washed out. A Scottish 10/- field glass of three mile power is a pleasant companion, so is a square of the ordnance map and a small pocket compass.

Compared with today's climbers, the visitors of the last century really did like roughing it. Who today would go onto

Snowdon without their waterproof jackets and trousers, good warm fleece jacket, at least two sweaters, often thermal underwear, and of course what Hughes for some reason missed out – good comfortable walking shoes, a day's supply of food and drink, first aid kit, and a whistle – all carried in a back-hugging comfortable rucksack?

By the early 1900s, there was such a good network of trains and coaches to the villages around Snowdon that more and more tourists came as day-trippers rather than to stay in the hotels, and made their own way up to the summit. The building of the Snowdon Mountain Railway also gave people the opportunity to reach the summit without even having to wear really protective clothing, and there was no longer the need for a guide up the Llanberis Path when one could just follow the train track (something which is no longer condoned). The accumulation of these twentieth century factors eventually negated the need for guides.

As for the present and the future, there are still local mountaineers that will take visitors up the paths to the summit of Snowdon, and they are usually found running local guest houses. Alternatively some of the outdoor equipment shops in Betws-y-coed, Llanberis or Capel Curig will give helpful advice, and the managers of the main hotels in the area still know someone or other who will help a visitor. There is also the National Park Warden Centre at Pen-y-pass where verbal information can be obtained about the various paths and the conditions underfoot (especially useful in winter), and also a general weather forecast for the day.

However, care should be taken with the modern usage of the term 'guide', and to ensure that you are accompanied by a proper qualified guide, you should contact the British Mountaineering Council in Manchester who can provide you with a list of their internationally qualified mountain guides, all of whom are members of the British Association of Mountain Guides.

Nowadays, walkers and climbers on Snowdon usually make their own way up the paths, either from their own map-reading capabilities, or from the many articles written in specialist monthly magazines, or one of the many guide books about Snowdonia. There are also many clubs and societies that can help visitors to Snowdon, both near the mountain such as The Snowdonia National Park Society based at Ty Hyll (the ugly house) at Betws-y-coed, or one of the hundreds of local climbing and walking clubs to be found all over the UK.

What is most important however, is that without a guide ore researched knowledge of the mountain, walkers and climbers should treat the massif with great care and respect. There is a well known saying: "The mountains are safe, it's the people who ascend them that are dangerous". As the highest peak in Wales, Snowdon attracts a great number of people who attempt to scale it by the various footpaths which lead to the summit. Most accidents can be avoided, and in analysing any accident, it can be attributed to one of three reasons: inexperience; a foolhardy action; or not having the proper equipment or footwear.

Having a railway running to its summit and a restaurant there, does tend to lure the public into a false sense of security, and on a good day it is the experience of a lifetime for most who ascend the mountain and feel the achievement of three or so hours of hard labour to stand on the top and admire the view. But despite the presence of man in many forms on the massif, all it needs is for nature to unfurl a thick blanket of cloud, some wind and some rain, and the ascent can change into a nightmare of man against a hostile environment.

The media often refer to a 'climber' injured on Snowdon, though the truth is more often that it is a 'walker' who is injured, but the editor gets more sensation in his report by reference to a climber. In fact, three quarters of mountain accidents can be attributed to holiday walkers rather than the more serious regular walkers and climbers, as the latter, on the whole, tend to be better equipped with proper protective equipment.

Even for the easy peaks, one should be equipped with the following items:

- Boots with a good tread pattern for the sole, and sturdy uppers to support and protect the feet.
- Rucksack to carry essential food and clothing.
- Wind and waterproof outer garments.
- Spare sweater or pile garment.
- Map, compass, torch, food, survival bag, and a first aid kit.

In the winter period, which on high ground can mean from November through to April, then the following should also be added:

- Ice axe, and pair of crampons.
- Extra warm clothing, gloves, and woollen hat.

In addition, a day's walk should be planned (which would include getting a weather forecast), and an early start made in winter to minimise coming down in the dark. Also, details of the planned route, together with the estimated time of return should be left with someone responsible who could give the necessary information to the rescue services.

Accidents most often occur to people on their descent when they are tired and possibly not concentrating. In the event of an accident, the injured person(s) should be made as comfortable as possible, the extent of the injuries diagnosed, and as much first aid as possible quickly administered. It is not often that people find themselves alone on Snowdon, providing they stick to the public paths, and whenever possible, somebody should remain with the injured person while a message is sent to alert the Rescue Services. That information must be of use, so it should include the time of the accident, location using six figure map references, injuries sustained, the prevailing weather conditions in that vicinity, and the equipment the injured person has available, for example a survival bag.

The police have the co-ordinating responsibility for getting aid to the injured. There are telephone call boxes near the starting points of all the public paths to the summit, and today most walkers carry a mobile phone. An emergency call to the police, giving the necessary information will set a rescue in motion which will usually involve the assistance of the local Mountain Rescue Team, civilian teams, and members of the Search and Rescue Dog Association.

The rescue of people from Snowdon has gone on over the years in many forms. Initially, it was by the walkers and climbers themselves with the aid of local farmers and quarrymen. Often in those days before the advent of specialised stretchers, a farm gate would be lifted from its hinges and used to convey the injured. However, it is hoped that the people who read this book and use the mountain will think about the risks that rescuers have to take, and not put themselves in situations that will require such help.

Climbing on Snowdon

As most of the historical books about Snowdon and Snowdonia adequately cover the stories and details of the exploits of the great men and women climbers that have visited the massif, I would rather readers obtained a copy of one or two of the books listed in the bibliography at the end of this book, and read at first hand of the thrills they had in the years gone by. Today, climbing is much more of a science, and I feel it is better dealt with in greater detail by the more specialised books available.

Suffice to say, some of the finest and most accessible climbs in the UK, and even in Europe, are to be found on Snowdon. Since the days of the early visitors, dramatic rock faces like those found on Y Lliwedd or Clogwyn Du'r Arddu have tested the skills and stamina of climbers, not forgetting also those less well publicised rocks found in Cwm Glas and around Dinas Mot. This section therefore contains just brief details of the main rock faces of the Snowdon massif so that at least this book can claim to be a comprehensive guide to the massif.

Clogwyn Du'r Arddu (SH599556)
Probably the best known rock-climbing area on Snowdon; it is often seen as the Climber's Paradise, and usually known as 'Cloggy'. It reaches up from Llyn Du'r Arddu to the west ridge off Snowdon leading into Cwm Brwynog and is divided into eight main climbing areas, the most impressive being the East Buttress.

Clogwyn y Ddysgl (SH616554)
This is a ridge that rises from Upper Cwm Glas to reach the summit of Crib y Ddysgl, and at its lower end is the famous Parson's Nose.

Craig Aderyn (SH639543)
A small crag situated just below Llyn Teyrn, near the pipeline in Upper Cwm Dyli. It is the southernmost of the two Teyrn Bluffs.

Craig y Rhaeadr (SH622562)

This crag is not as popular as others on Snowdon, so often you can get the place to yourself. It has a waterfall that cascades down it even in summer, and which makes the rocks very slippery. In winter, the whole crag becomes covered in thick ice.

Crib Goch (SH625553)

This area of rock also rises from the screes of Upper Cwm Glas, and joins the summit of the Crib Goch pinnacle ridge.

Dinas Mot (SH627563)

Dinas Mot is the large cliff found at the end of the north ridge off Crib Goch. Its main attraction is the large triangular area of slab at its centre, commonly called the 'nose'. On its right is the Western Wing, split by two gullies, and on the left is the Eastern Wing – a towering buttress with lots of overhangs.

Gyrn Las (SH613559)

This cliff is quite close to Craig y Rhaeadr, and dominates Cwm Glas Mawr from where it rises. It is divided into three buttresses, and being a more popular crag, tends to be busy.

Llechog (SH597537)

This cliff lies north-facing in Cwm Clogwyn, and is best reached via the Rhyd Ddu Path. Although it looks very dangerous, in fact it consists of a maze of short slabs interspersed with grassy ledges.

Y Lliwedd (SH623534)

One of the most awe-inspiring climbing cliffs on Snowdon. It is almost half a mile wide, and rises 1000 feet up from Llyn Llydaw to form one half of the Snowdon Horseshoe. The whole cliff is divided into four main buttresses, and they are often very wet which can make climbing difficult, but there are also a number of grass ledges on which climbers can rest.

Nature on Snowdon

Initially I planned to link the various plants and animals to the habitats found on or near the main routes up to the summit. However, after discussions with both the National Park Authority and the Countryside Council for Wales, I decided that as the area is now a nature reserve, and in the interests of nature, it would be more appropriate to simply itemise some the flora and fauna found within the various habitats, thus avoiding the possibility of walkers leaving the proper paths attempting to find a specific species.

I hope therefore that the readers will understand this and that it will not detract from the book as a guide to the nature of the massif. Similarly, in such a short guide, it is impossible to list every plant and animal to be found on Snowdon. Consequently I have included a selection that will give an overall impression of the environment. Furthermore, to make it easier for the walker and climber to relate to their natural surroundings, the plants and animals are discussed within the habitats in which they are usually found, rather than by type.

The lowlands and semi-upland meadows of Snowdon used to have an abundance of wild flowers prior to the modernisation of farming – ploughing, drainage and fertilising. Now, even down near Gwynant or Llanberis, it is almost impossible to find a meadow with its old flora intact. In the more acidic fields, variety tends to be taken over by buttercups. However it is still possible to find such distinguished plants as whorled caraway, petty whin, ivy-leaved bellflower, devil's-bit scabious, and bog pimpernel. On the other hand, the more lime-rich meadows are strongholds of such plants as twayblade, quaking grass, bitter vetch, saw-wort, globeflower, wood spotted orchid, and fragrant orchid with occasionally the rarer species such as melancholy thistle, wood horsetail, moonwort, and adder's tongue.

Nearer the farms more common plants are to be found such as comfrey, Welsh poppy, spindle, burdock, slender speedwell, greater celandine, fennel, soapwort, wormwood, gout-weed, and Good King Henry. On the more open land plants such as small, and pale toadflaxes, apetalous pearlwort, rose-bay willow herb, lamb's lettuce, and evening primrose can be found.

The plant which causes most concern is the rhododendron, which is now taking a hold on the slopes in the Gwynant valley in the lane at the start of the Watkin path, for instance. Thankfully the National Trust and other volunteers are well deployed in clearing it before it takes too much of a hold and becomes a pest, especially in the areas where bracken is most abundant. In some ways even the bracken, a form of which may have been part of the undergrowth of the primeval forests of Snowdon, is seen as a pest by some farmers. Although it provides a wonderfully colourful sight on the slopes in the autumn, some argue that the land would be put to better use as pasture. In addition to the slopes, bracken is also present in the one or two lower woods, and in some places other ferns such as male fern, broad buckler fern, and lady fern, are also found.

Five thousand years ago, much of the lower parts of Snowdon were covered by broad-leaved trees, but today the one or two woods that remain are mainly sessile oak, with some alder, ash, and birch. The soils of these woods are predominantly acidic, and sustain such plants as wood sage, wood-sorrel, slender St. John's-wort, foxglove, common cow-wheat, and sometimes bluebells. However where there is slightly less acidity, herb-robert, wood anemone, red campion, lesser celandine, ivy-leaved speedwell, bugle and wood speedwell can also exist. In the autumn, such woods are also abundant with toadstools, bracket fungi, puffballs, and other fungi.

As the slopes rise above the lowlands, the woods and meadows are replaced by the vast undulating grassland that covers most of the Snowdon massif. Here and there it gives way to rock or heather-moorland or patches of rushes, but generally this turf forms the cover of the mountain, and contributes much to the beauty of upland Snowdon. In fact, the seasonal changes so noticeable on the mountain scenery because of the colour changes of these plants, which dominate areas of the landscape extensive enough to be visible from distance.

Though it may be supposed that in all this vast acreage of grassland there would be found a large number of species, the actual number is extremely small. Of the hundreds of grasses, just four predominate: the sheep's fescue, common bent, mat-grass, and purple moor-grass, merely because they are so perfectly adapted to acidic mountain soils. One or two other grasses such as wavy hair-grass and tufted hair-grass can be found in abundant patches, and the moor sedge, yellow-flowered tormentil, white-flowered heath bestraw, and vari-coloured heath milk-wort are also found on the higher slopes, but very few others have managed to combat the blanket of these commonest grasses.

Another major type of habitat found on the higher land of Snowdon is the peat bog, which can cover large areas of the land, especially on flat or hollow ground in the wide shallow saucers that were occupied by lakes in the post-glacial period, but that have since been choked by vegetation. These bogs can be recognised from miles away by the blackness of the bare peat and the dark mantle of heather interspersed with white islands of cotton-grass. Where the peat is deepest, wettest, and most acid, the bright green or sometimes reddish spaghnum or bog mosses can be found, forming what walkers often call 'bog-holes'. Other plants that flourish in these adverse habitats are bog asphodel with its brilliant yellow spikes, and cranberry that creeps about the surface of the bog mosses.

In bog pools that are not completely choked with sphagnum, the insectivorous bladderwort is often found, and surrounding the bogs, deer-sedge commonly flourishes. In fact where the bogs merge into slightly less acid but still wet ground, there is an immediate increase in the number of plants to be found in greater abundance, such as the lesser spearwort, marsh violet, marsh speedwell, marsh pennywort, and devil's-bit scabious. The edges of such bogs are also the domain of the aptly named tussock sedge whose growth in clumps is often another obstacle to walkers who stray from the footpaths.

To get the most pleasure out of the plant life on the higher slopes and summit ridges of Snowdon, you should have, or try to develop, an eye for the rock types that exist on the massif. This does not mean that you have to be a qualified geologist, but it does help to understand that some types of rock are far richer in plants than others, and as Louis Pasteur once remarked: "In the spheres of observation, chance favours the prepared mind", in other words, if you know where to look, the chances of finding what you're looking for are greater.

The most obvious feature of the summit flora is the relative lack of both species and number of plants, and when one considers the climatic conditions on these high parts, it is perhaps surprising that any plants exist there at all. Even the sheep cause havoc with the plants on these parts, as in many cases they replace grass as their staple diet.

The plant most usually found on the higher rock faces is the woolly-haired moss, which can make a luxurious green-grey blanket amongst the rocks. The decay of this moss probably contributes most of the thin humus that collects amongst the stones and rock fissures, and therefore allows the establishment of other plants such as the parsley fern, crowberry, bilberry, and other summit species. Two of the common club mosses, the alpine and the fir, are also prolific on these higher parts of the massif, as are the common bent, viviparous fescue, annual meadow-grass, and mat-grass.

Of the sedge family, the stiff sedge is the one found on the high ground, and only a few of the ferns reach such exposed parts, and even then are normally found in crevices out of the wind, beech fern, hard fern, lady fern, and the broad buckler being the most common. The only other plant type found on these acidic rocks is the green lichen which forms patches on the weathered rock.

But the mountain plants that are cherished by most of the botanists, amateur naturalists, and general walkers and climbers are those classified as the Arctic-alpines. They are mostly to be found on the cliffs just below the summits and are restricted to rocks that are rich in lime. They can neatly be divided into two categories – the abundant, and the rare. Of the former, the most common one is the purple saxifrage, whose bright magenta flowers can often be seen amongst the snows of late winter. Some time later, the white flowered starry and mossy saxifrages then bloom, along with other plants such as the alpine meadow-rue, moss campion, spring sandwort, and mountain sorrel.

Of the rare varieties found on the mountain ledges, the alpine chickweed, arctic chickweed, hoary whillow grass, northern bedstraw, arctic saxifrage, mountain avens, alpine cinquefoil, alpine saw-wort, and alpine meadow-grass, all can be found crowded together on the lime-rich cliffs. But the most distinguished arctic-alpine found on the massif has to be the Snowdon lily, whose scientific name (*Lloydia serotina*) commemorates Edward Lhuyd (or Lloyd) who discovered it in 1682. This tiny white lily which flowers in late May – early June, is no more than 4 inches tall, and when not in flower, the grass-like leaves easily lose themselves among the neighbouring plants. Fortunately, it is no longer found in accessible places, so its extinction has at least been temporarily halted.

As mentioned at the beginning of this chapter, the National Park Authority especially requests that visitors respect the plants found on the massif, so although this chapter provides an insight into the wonderful selection of plants that can be seen whilst walking on the mountain, I hope that readers of this book will help to ensure that they will remain there for future generations to appreciate too.

With regard to fauna, among the animals of the lowlands, probably the most noticeable are the sheep, now almost the 'mascot' of Wales, and the one animal still farmed on the massif. The other most numerous mammals are the rabbits which can be seen around most of the lower slopes, together with, on rare occasions, the brown hare, foxes and the mountain goats.

In the moist and warm habitats of the lower slopes and woods the slow-worm is found, though by day they normally hide under stones or vegetation. Other nocturnal creatures include frogs, toads, mice, voles, and shrews living in the woods and grasslands.

As the result of its rarity and its beauty, the pine-martin is surely Snowdon's most distinguished mammal, but not only is it nocturnal, it is also hardly ever seen on the massif, unlike during Pennant's time, when it was so abundant that its fur was much used for the linings of magistrates' gowns. Polecats are also rare visitors to the massif, though they are quite abundant in other parts of Snowdonia. And no longer can you see the red deer, nor the wild cats that used to roam the lowlands many years ago.

Probably the most observed animals of not only the lowlands, but all over the massif are the birds, and even though they are free to fly all over the area, they have their preferences as regards where on the mountain they are normally to be found.

Among with the birds most commonly seen flying around the mountains, the raven must be the one that most people recognise, and they are to be seen even in the most severe weather when most of the other species have retreated to more sheltered places. These birds produce a variety of strange noises that accompany the aerial tricks that easily identify them, the most common being for the bird to turn upside down in mid-air after which it may glide for several yards breast upwards. When soaring normally, ravens look very much like a black cross in the sky, and when using their wings to gain height, make an easily identifiable whooshing sound.

The other black bird to be seen high in the mountains is the chough, which is easily identified by its red beak and legs, and also its individualistic chee-ow call. These birds are not as common as the ravens, and are often mistaken for jackdaws.

Until recently, peregrine falcons were also commonly seen at the summit, but now they are a rare sight, due to the huge decrease in numbers caused by the use of pesticides on the crops eaten by the smaller birds on which the peregrines feed. So by way of their food-chain, these marvellous birds ingest the poison and have died in large numbers. So far, however, the kestrels of the uplands have not suffered the same plight as the peregrines, mainly because of their different feeding habits, namely to eat insect-feeding birds such as the pipits and larks, rather than the seed-eating species.

Another large bird often seen foraging on the mountain-side is the carrion crow, which is certainly unpopular with farmers as it has a tendency to attack weak sheep and lambs, and tear out their eyes. The only other upland bird of prey that is very rarely seen is the merlin, although until well into the late nineteenth century it was a frequent visitor to the massif.

A bird more often heard than seen is the ring ouzel, especially the cock. Found mainly among rocks and heather, it also inhabits the old slate quarries and abandoned mine buildings. Although they advertise themselves by their chattering alarm cries, or pleasant song, ring ouzels are in fact very secretive, often hiding behind rocks.

The smallest of the birds found on Snowdon, the wren, is probably the hardiest and has an ability to withstand even the worst mountain winters. When the ground is frozen and all the other birds have retreated to the warmer lowlands, the wren can be found hopping around the highest ledges. Their survival is thought to lie in their cave-dwelling habits, as these birds can live in damp cavities under rocks where there exists a humid climate even though the outside is freezing. This is due to the fact that the water that seeps down into these sheltered crevices never freezes and in them can be found spiders, woodlice, and other small creatures that are food to the wren. It is therefore no coincidence that the Latin name for the wren is *Troglodytes* – the cave-dweller.

In the nesting season, another bird often shares the boulders and screes with the wren, the wheatear, which can be found on ground anywhere between 800 and 2,000 feet. Wheatears are normally found on stretches of cropped turf scattered with boulders, the former so that they can run on it to catch insects, and the latter so that they can perch on them as vantage points and also places from which to sing. They are quite dependent on the mountain sheep to keep the grass short, and are often seen along the side of moorland tracks that are in frequent use by farm animals whose droppings attract a large number of the insects on which the wheatears feed.

The mountain slopes would also be rather quiet places without the pipits flitting from place to place with their endless singing. During the summer months they are found all over the massif, flying up from the ground where they have been resting in the hollows they shape in the grass. The most abundant species is the meadow pipit which inhabits most of the grassland, heather, bracken, rushes, and bogs, and being insect eaters are mainly found from spring to early autumn.

In mid to late April, the male cuckoo arrives to frequent areas between about 600 and 1500 feet. Throughout May and June they can be seen flying along the same short stretches often being chased by wheatears or pipits, then within a very short period around about the end of July, the adults depart for Africa, leaving the young to be fed and looked after by their foster-parents.

Perhaps the most graceful bird to frequent the massif is the curlew whose arrival is announced by their characteristic song in late February and early March. Unfortunately, they are not a common sight on the massif, in comparison with other areas of Snowdonia, but their presence is always welcomed by walkers, not only for their wonderful looks, but for the marvellous range of notes they sing, ranging from the short 'courlee' to almost triumphant wailings.

The only other birds found on Snowdon with any regularity are the pied and grey wagtails, normally from spring to autumn. The grey variety with its brilliant yellow underparts is usually restricted to streams, while the more abundant black and white pied wagtail is also to be found around rocky areas, and is also a great visitor of upland farms. Often, in places where grey wagtails exist, dippers can be found too, though they are much less common.

Quite a number of other birds enjoy a brief summer on the mountains when there is a plentiful supply of insects, seeding grasses, and abundant fruit on plants such as bilberries. Woodpigeons, thrushes, warblers, finches, and rooks can all usually be seen at some time or other on the massif, and in August, even the herring gulls move up from the coast in large flocks, not so much for food, but to moult. Foraging is left to the gulls which are now almost residents on the summit, enjoying the left-overs from the sandwiches, crisps, cakes, and anything else they are given by the visitors on the top.

With this extensive variety of bird life on the massif, one can't help imagining what it must have been like for the first climbers and walkers to hear the flapping of the huge wings, and the gushing noise that would have been made by an eagle soaring around Yr Wyddfa, when it truly was Eryri.

Some Legendary Places on Snowdon

Although the whole of the area around Snowdon is steeped with legends, and many of the lakes or cwms have intriguing meanings when translated from Welsh into English, there are some places on the massif that have specific legends that are worth listing individually, as they will assist in the overall appreciation of many of the walks that have been described in this book. To enable walkers to easily identify their position on the massif, map grid references have been provided for each one.

Bwlch y Gwyddyl (SH 655554)

This name translates as the Irishmen's Pass, and is the site of an ancient Irish settlement. Legend has it that a pile of treasure is buried here but only an Irishman will be successful in finding it.

Bwlch y Saethau (SH 615542)

Translated it means the Pass of the Arrows, and local legend states that when King Arthur had vanquished his foes in the old city of Tregalan (at the head of Cwm y Llan), he drove them over this pass into Cwm Dyli. However, when he reached the top of the pass himself, the enemy let fly a shower of arrows, and Arthur was fatally wounded. In fact, in older manuscripts, authors have made reference to an old cairn that stood either on the pass, or a little to the south of it.

Folklore was not content to leave the legend unfinished, and tells of what happened to Arthur's followers. It appears that they retreated to the precipices of Lliwedd and there found shelter in a cave, inaccessible to all but the most daring of climbers. There, the 'lads of Eryri' (*llanciau Eryri*) await the day when Arthur will return to triumph, and again give victory to the Brythonic race.

Cwm Dyli (SH 635543)

The word 'dyli' or 'dylir' signifies 'a flood', and the cwm has long been known as the valley of rushing waters due to the view of the waterfalls that used to be visible from the Beddgelert road.

Cwm Llan (SH 616523)

The valley through which the Watkin Path passes on the route to Snowdon's summit. As well as being the legendary site of the old city of Tregalan, it is also supposed to be the area in which the *Tylwyth Teg* or 'little people' live.

A shepherd is supposed to have heard a wailing sound whilst walking in the valley, and found one of the *Tylwyth Teg* trapped by a large boulder, which he moved to set the fairy free. Later, two old men came and thanked him, and gave him a walking stick. From that time onwards, every sheep in his flock bore two ewe lambs until he unfortunately lost the stick some years later in a flood, and his luck vanished with it.

Glaslyn (SH 615545)

The blue or green lake, given its name from the striking colour it has taken due to the presence of ore from the old copper mines. The old name for this lake was Llyn y Ffynnon Las ('The Lake of the Green Well), and has a most sinister reputation in folklore, as well as being an uncanny place to be in the swirling mists that often shroud its shores.

The legend linked to Glaslyn is that it is the abode of demons, is bottomless, harbours no ordinary fish, and never freezes (except in the coldest winters: see page 79). Furthermore, any living creature venturing into it comes to a speedy end, and no bird will fly over its eerie waters. Stories are told of some of its gruesome inhabitants being hooked by unaware anglers, who in the event have never waited to see the full detail of their catch.

The most famous of all its legendary dwellers is the great *afanc*, monster from the pool on the Conwy near the Fairy Glen which is still called Llyn Yr Afanc. The monster was dragged out from its original home, drawn across the mountains of Dolwyddelan by a chain attached to two oxen, and then let loose on the shores of Llyn y Ffynnon Las into which it disappeared, and to this day still lives. A shepherd in the early eighteenth century, who claimed to have seen the monster, described it as "toadlike and with tails and wings". They said that it also made horrible shrieking noises, so walkers on the Miners' Track – beware!

Llyn Du'r Arddu (SH 601557)

The literal translation is the 'Black Lake of Arddu', though it is more of a pool than a lake, lying beneath the steep black cliffs of Clogwyn Du'r Arddu. These cliffs are a favourite challenge for the more adventurous climbers that visit Snowdon, but the spot has a strange and creepy atmosphere. No wonder the lake is said to be haunted, and is associated with stories of fairies and goblins dancing on its shores.

Llyn y Gadair (SH 538522)

Literally translated this is the 'Lake of the Chair', but the legend attached to this lake near Rhyd-ddu on the southern side of Snowdon, is that of a terrible golden-haired monster that was rumoured to live in a lair near close by. It caused a great deal of mischief in the neighbourhood until it was chased up the pass of Drws-y-coed and slain. A tale is also told of a man in the eighteenth century who swam across the lake and at the halfway point was seen to be followed by a long trailing object which, as he neared the shore, enveloped him in its great coiled body, and dragged him into a deep hole at the mouth of a nearby stream.

Llyn Llydaw (SO 630545)

There are no clear cut translations of *llydaw*. Some historians think that it is derived from *lludw* or 'ashes', from the presence of a certain amount of ashy material along its shore, both from the natural geological rocks that are present now, and also from the previous discoveries of the refuse of copper smeltings.

Llydaw has also been translated as extending along the water, and also 'coastland', both of which would link in with the fact that not only have the remains of lakeside dwellings been found there, but a prehistoric canoe was also found in the mud when the lake was drained during the construction of the causeway. There is a further theory that Llydaw is simply a proper name attributed to a person living near the lake in the past.

Irrespective of the derivation you wish to select, when you next visit the shores of Llyn Llydaw, why not think of the picture that Sir Rhys Jones conjures up when he writes:

...below was Llyn Llydaw with its sequestered isle, connected then by means only of a primitive canoe with a shore occupied by men engaged in working the ore of Eryri. Nay, with the eyes of Malory we seem to watch Bedivere making, with Excalibur in his hands, his three reluctant journeys to the lake ere he yielded it to the arm emerging from the deep.

We fancy we behold how "eyn fast by the bank houed a lytyl barge with many fayre ladyes in it", which was to carry the wounded Arthur away to the accompaniment of mourning and loud lamentation." But the legend of the Marchlyn bids us modify Malory's language as to the barge containing many ladies all wearing black hoods, and take our last look at the warrior departing rather in a coracle with three wonderously fair women attending to his wounds.

Llyn Teyrn (SO 642545)
This, according to the majority of Welsh historians, is the Lake of the Tyrant or Ruler though there is no tradition linked to a specific person, either legendary or actual. It is thought to have been a place where, in folklore, the princes that lived at Beddgelert used to fish, hence the link to rulers (and perhaps also tyrants).

Nant Gwynant (SH 628512)
The old name for this valley was Nanhwynen, or Nanhwynan, and the source of the word *gwynant* is thought to have come from a personal name such as Gwynen, Gwynan or Gwynain, all linked to Arthurian legends. Most Welsh writers in fact adopt the form 'Nant Gwynen', and the only reference to the older name is found in the *Triads*, in which there is a reference to a meeting in 'Nanhwynain' between Medrawd and Iddawg Corn Prydain, "plotting to encompass the downfall of Arthur".

Llwyd wrote that "At Nanhwynen trees were so thick that a man on a white horse could not be seen from Llyn Dinas to Penygwryd, except in two places, and one of these has ever since been called, Goleugoed."

Y Lliwedd (SH 625532)

The word signifies the state of being stained or coloured, a term which in fact would be equally applicable to any of the cliffs in the Snowdon Horseshoe. A more realistic translation would appear to be derived from *llif*, or *lli* (a flood), and gwedd (aspect). The cave referred to relating to Arthur's men (*Ogof Llanciau Eryri*), according to another story, is on the left-hand side near the top of Llyn Llydaw, and one day, a shepherd trying to rescue one of his sheep from a ledge nearby, inadvertently found the opening to the cave, and entered to find row upon row of Arthur's warriors, resting on their shields, awaiting his return.

The shepherd accidentally hit his head on a great bell hanging in the entrance of the cave, the clanging of which awakened the men, which needless to say gave the shepherd the shock of his life. He is supposed to have fled at great haste from the cave, and was "never the same man again"!

Yr Wyddfa (SH 610544)

Various translations have been given to this name, one of which is place of presence owing to the Bardic meetings that were once thought to have taken place on the summit. Sir John Rhys in his *Celtic Folklore* published in 1901 favours the meaning tomb or barrow especially in relation to the legend of the giant Rhita, sometimes known as Rhica, who killed kings and then clothed himself in a garment made from their beards. Prior to the buildings being erected on the summit, just a cairn existed there, which local people called *Carnedd y Cawr*, which translated means the 'giant's cairn'. The cairn had also been known as *Gwyddfa Rhita* (Rhita's Cairn). A more realistic translation however, probably derives from the mention in the Aberconwy charter of *Wedduavaur*, which relates to "the great [or important] tumulus".

The Custodians of Snowdon

Snowdon lies in one of the earliest formed National Parks, and it is worth remembering what G.M. Trevelyan wrote in the foreword to the document produced in 1938 that put forward the initial idea of such parks:

> The Government undertakes to assist the health of the nation and to find playing fields for the dwellers in the vast cities to play cricket and football. But it is no less essential, for any national health scheme, to preserve for the nation walking grounds and regions where young and old can enjoy the sight of unspoiled nature.
>
> And it is not a question of physical exercise only, it is also a question of spiritual values. Without sight of the beauty of nature the spiritual power of the British people will be atrophied!

Since that original report was published, many millions of 'city dwellers' have visited the various National Parks, and it has been necessary to ensure that such areas are kept not only for the existing population, but also for future generations. To quote the famous saying: "National Parks are not ours, but ours to look after".

Snowdon itself is not only a part of the Snowdonia National Park, it is also a National Nature Reserve in its own right, and it is therefore even more important that the land be preserved and maintained to keep the habitat as stable as possible.

To ensure that Snowdon is preserved, three 'custodians' are responsible for it. Two of these have been appointed by the Government – The Snowdonia National Park Authority (Parc Cenedlaethol Eryri), and The Countryside Council for Wales (Cyngor Cefn Gwlad Cymru). The third is a society that has been formed by ordinary people who have concern for the area and act as more of a watchdog group – The Snowdonia National Park Society (*Cymdeithas Parc Cenedlaethol Eryri*).

The land that makes up the Snowdon massif is privately owned by a number of farmers and the National Trust, which, after a mammoth fundraising 'Snowdon Appeal' in 1997-98 bought the largest farm: Hafod-y-Llan, which covers 2,500 acres (1012 hectares). The Trust also owns the neighbouring farm of Hafod y Porth (to the west) which is run on a shared basis with a local farmer. There are neighbouring farms, Gwastadannas to the east and Fridd Uchaf and Clogwyn y Gwin to the north. The Welsh Assembly Government still owns 300 acres of land along the summit ridge of Snowdon over to Crib y Ddisgl.

Perhaps the most difficult task that the National Park Authority has is the maintenance of the public footpaths on the massif. Being in exposed areas, especially the higher sections, they tend to be eroded by the natural forces of rain, wind, snow and ice. When the boots of millions of walkers over the years are added to this erosion, one can imagine the problems that exist. Erosion means to eat away; gradually destroy; wear out; and that is what is happening on many upland areas of Snowdon.

Before the surge of walkers taking to the hills for recreation, the odd quarry track or sheep track was used to accommodate the few mountaineers that ventured to the uplands, but due to the improved individual mobility, new roads, and the countryside being used for educational and 'character-building' purposes, these tracks can no longer withstand the pressure. Furthermore, when one narrow track became filled with water and mud, walkers would start walking on the grass at the side of the old track. When this too became muddy, another new track would be made, eventually the width of the original track becomes yards rather than feet. For this reason it is important for visitors not to stray from these paths, otherwise even more erosion will take place, and the wardens and their staff will not physically be able to cope with the drastic results. It is even more essential that other forms of human erosion such as cycling and other forms of transport, are also controlled.

One might think that a mountain such as Snowdon is so hard that it could withstand almost anything, but this is not so. It is surprisingly fragile, and has to be protected for both the sake of the physical landscape and the wildlife that exists on it. For the last three decades the Authority has undertaken positive projects in an attempt to prevent the erosion scars from becoming wider and deeper The work was initially done with the aid of unpaid volunteers, but latterly European funding has allowed the various custodians to employ staff and monitor the efforts of volunteers.

It is often taken for granted by visitors that such repair work will be done, and that it is nothing to do with them. Indeed it has even been suggested that it is what is expected! But I wonder how many of these erosion-producing visitors consider those who have actually to carry out this very hard maintenance work. Reaching the damaged sites is hard enough, but having to work at the end of a long walk in bad weather must be one of the most demanding jobs there is. So next time you may think of crossing over a fence to take a short-cut, or move a few stones to add to a cairn, or walk off a muddy path not to dirty your shoes, just think of the footpath workers.

There is a National Park policy which says that conservation should come before public enjoyment if there is a conflict, but striking a balance between wildlife and people is much preferred. However, as the massif becomes more popular, there is really only one way of being sure that it can stand up to the pressure of this popularity , and that is to put it first.

It is not only the land that has to be maintained. We often forget that Snowdon is not an unoccupied open space to 'play in'. Farmers still work the land, and their property, in the form of fences and gates has to be cared for. Likewise, there is the property of the inhabitants of past eras such as the old mine ruins, all of which make up the totality of the experience gained whilst walking on the mountain.

Although the area around Snowdon was first recommended for conservation in 1947, it was in 1962 that the Nature Conservancy Council opened active discussions with the National Park Authority and the various landowners with a view to protecting the natural habitat of the massif by nominating it as a National Nature Reserve. The initial reaction was one of surprise as the area, almost 6,000 acres, was used intensively by walkers and climbers who at first imagined that they would be banned. An uproar in the press resulted. But research showed that over 90% of visitors actually stayed on the recognised paths and once walkers knew there was no intention to curtail their activities providing they adhered to these public tracks, any real potentially adverse reaction disappeared.

The initial plans proposed more of an open access agreement from the landowners who in turn would benefit from the protection under Nature Reserve rules, and in 1964 Mr P.H.O.Williams who owned the land at Hafod y Llan on the south (Beddgelert) side of the massif, became the first to agree to such a new arrangement. In 1966, the two other major landowners – Sir Richard Bulkely and Mr W.O. Williams also agreed to have their land 'protected', and the National Nature Reserve came into being.

Many of the plants growing on the land of the massif have survived because of the remoteness of Snowdon, whereas in many lowland areas man has found it easier to destroy the natural habitat. Hence some of the most extreme rock faces sustain the environments that allow the very rare alpine plants to thrive. And it is worth remembering that these plants are the direct descendants of those that the early botanists of the eighteenth century would have seen, which proves that conservation can and does work, and that we should always be thinking of how best to retain these specimens for our future generation to see.

Many times over the last hundred or so years, plans have been put forward which would have had a disastrous effect on the continuity of the preservation of this unique habitat. Some have been prevented, such as the plan for a cable car to the summit; or an underground hotel there; or a power station in Cwm-y-Llan fed through a tunnel under Lliwedd! Others have succeeded as can evidenced by the overland Cwm Dyli pipeline which campaigners tried unsuccessfully to have put underground and out of sight, when it was recently refurbished. It is with such plans that the SNPS gets involved, putting forward the 'people's' voice, and acts as an essential balance to ensure that governmental decisions do take every aspect into consideration when looking at the various potentially destructive plans.

But it is the people themselves that will eventually decide what happens to the preservation of this great place. The more visitors that arrive on the massif, the harder it will be to maintain the equilibrium that is so essential to the natural habitat. The more boots that tread the paths, the harder it will be for the Wardens to maintain them. And above all else there is the overriding question of finance. Who will pay for the upkeep of this unique environment?

It is apparent that insufficient government funds are allocated for the general upkeep of the massif, but we often forget that other parts of the National Park have to be cared for too, even though they don't receive as many visitors. Some years ago, it was even suggested that one of the organisations responsible for looking after the massif researched the feasibility of charging visitors to walk there. Thankfully the research never took place.

No doubt only a few walkers and climbers now object to the government funding of the National Parks or even such landowners as the National Trust charging a membership fee to help pay for the increased access and also the prevention of 'people erosion'; which in some ways can be argued is a form of paying for access – it's just a politically different way of doing it.

Whatever will happen, I am sure it will be for the best to ensure the continued preservation of what must be the most magnificent geological and picturesque mountain in the Principality, and I hope in some way that this book will provide the reasons why this should be the case. If Snowdon is to survive it will be necessary on occasion to say: "No, that cannot be allowed". This will be neither to deny people their fundamental liberty, nor to spoil their enjoyment. It is a matter of discouraging them from doing things that may destroy Snowdon, so that there will be a Snowdon to enjoy.

A Snowdon Timeline

1639   First recorded ascent of Snowdon by Thomas Johnson using the Beddgelert route from Caernarfon.

1682   Survey by Caswell sets height at 3720ft.

1773   Pennant ascends Snowdon from Llanberis via Bwlch Maesgwm and Du'r Arddu ridge and sets height at 3568ft.

1795   Snowdon copper mines first opened.

1801   Horse-path made from Gorphwysfa to Glaslyn mines.

1801   A cottage was built on the site of the Penygwryd hotel, by John Roberts of Llanberis.

1819   First shelter built on Snowdon.

1827   Cairn erected on Snowdon summit by Ordnance Survey.

1830   New road built to replace old track to Llanberis.

1831   First recorded ascent via Pig Track and Bwlch-y-moch.

1838   First true hut built on summit, and Thomas Roscoe climbed to summit from Cwm Dyli via Llydaw and zig-zags on Miners' Track.

1846   Mr and Mrs Hammer spend honeymoon on summit.

1847   Harry Owen purchases Penygwryd and acts as guide up Snowdon.

1853   Llydaw water level lowered and causeway built.

1854   George Borrow climbed Snowdon via Llanberis Path, and party held on summit to celebrate the coming of age of Edward Bulkeley Williams, heir to Baron Hill estate.

1856   Prehistoric canoe discovered in Llyn Llydaw, and miners' barracks built at Llyn Teyrn.

1869   Railway from Caernarfon to Llanberis opened.

1873   New dam built at Glaslyn, and first Ward-Lock series guide book published.

1881   Railway opened from Caernarfon to South Snowdon (Rhyd-ddu).

1884   First ascent to summit on bicycle (penny-farthing).

1886   C. Taylor taken to summit, aged two and a half days!

1887	Bonfire lit and entertainments on summit to celebrate Queen Victoria's Golden Jubilee.
1892	Sir Edward Watkin opened path from Nant Gwynant.
1896	Snowdon Mountain Railway opened.
1898	Brittania Copper Mine Ltd built mill at Llyn Llydaw.
1901	Pen-y-pass hotel rebuilt, and North Wales branch of BMA hold celebratory dinner on summit.
1904	First ascent to summit by car .
1906	Cwm Dyli power station opened.
1912	First ascent to summit by motorcycle.
1916	Last copper mine on Snowdon closed.
1924	Man on motorbike makes fastest ascent to summit.
1925	H.S. Carr survived three days in Cwm Glas, roped to his dead companion.
1936	New summit station and hotel built.
1940	Snowdon Ranger Hotel acquired by YHA.
1942	Wartime occupation of summit hotel by Ministry, and end to residential use.
1971	Pen-y-pass hotel opened as new YHA hostel.
1977	Proposed bonfire on Crib-y-ddysgl to celebrate Queen's Silver Jubilee cancelled due to bad weather (snow in June!)
1978	H.L. Thackwell from America climbed to summit to celebrate his ninetieth birthday. Causeway rebuilt across Llyn Llydaw by National Park staff.
1981	Propane gas fire lit at Clogwyn Station to commemorate wedding of H.R.H. The Prince of Wales and Lady Diana.
1984	National Trust's first Snowdon Marathon – on roads around the mountain.
1989	Snowdon summit hotel refurbished, and new Cwm Dyli pipeline constructed.
1998	Sir Anthony Hopkins donated £1 million to help buy Hafod y Llan farm as part of the National Trust's 'Save Snowdon' appeal.
2006	Snowdon summit building demolished. Summit bare of buildings for the first time in a hundred and seventy years.

Useful Addresses

Cambrian Ornithological Society (Cymdeithas Adarydda Cambria), Pen-y-Ffridd, Llangernyw, Abergele LL22 8RH. Tel. 01745 860279, http://mysite.wanadoo-members.co.uk/cambrianos

Council for National Parks (Cyngor y Parciau Cenedlaethol), 6-7 Barnard Mews, London, SW11 1QU. Tel. 020 7924 4077, http://www.cnp.org.uk/

Countryside Council for Wales (Cyngor Cefn Gwlad Cymru), Maes-y-Ffynnon, Penrhosgarnedd, Bangor, Gwynedd LL57 2DW. Tel. 08451 306 229, http://www.ccw.gov.uk

Forestry Commission Wales (Comisiwn Coedwigaeth Cymru), Victoria House, Victoria Terrace, Aberystwyth Ceredigion SY23 2DQ. Tel: 0845 604 0845, http://www.forestry.gov.uk/wales

National Trust (Ymddiriedolaeth Genedlaethol Cymru), Trinity Square, Llandudno, Gwynedd, LL30 2DE. Tel: 01492 8601231, http://www.nationaltrust.org.uk/main/w-global/w-localtoyou/w-wales.htm

National Mountain Centre (Canolfan Fynydd Genedlaethol), Plas-y-Brenin, Capel Curig, Betws-y-coed, Conwy, LL24 OET. Tel. 01690 720214. http://www.pyb.co.uk

Royal Society for the Protection of Birds (Wales Office), Sutherland House, Castlebridge, Cowbridge Road East, Cardiff, CF11 9AB. Tel: 02920 353000. http://www.rspb.org.uk/wales

Snowdonia National Park Authority (Parc Cenedlaethol Eryri), Penrhyndeudraeth, Gwynedd, LL48 6LF. Telephone: 01766 770274. http://www.eryri-npa.gov.uk

Snowdonia Society (Cymdeithas Eryri), Ty Hyll, Capel Curig, Conwy LL24 0DS. Tel: 01690 720287. http://www.snowdonia-society.org.uk

Welsh Place-Name Elements

aber, mouth, confluence
afon, river, stream
allt, hillside
annedd, dwelling
ar, upon
aran, mountain
arth, hill

bach, small
bala, outlet of lake
ban (pl *bannau*), summit
banc, hill
bere, kite, buzzard
berfedd, middle
betws, oratory
beudy, cowshed
big, peak
blaen (pl *blaenau*), head of valley
bod, dwelling
bont, bridge
bras, prominent
bro, region, vale
bron, rounded hill
brwynog, rushy
bryn, hill
bwlch, pass
bychan, small

cader (*cadair*), chair, fortress
cae, field
caer, fort
cafn, trough
cain, beautiful
can (*cant*), a hundred
canol, middle
capel, chapel
carn, *carnedd* (pl *carneddau*), heap

of stones,
cairn, mountain
carreg, rock
castell, castle
cefn, ridge
celli, grove
ceunant, ravine
cil (pl *ciliau*), nook
clawdd (pl *cloddiau*), embankment
clegyr, crag
clogwyn, cliff
coch, red
coed, woodland
corlan, sheep-fold
cors, bog
craig (pl *creigiau*), rock
crib (pl *cribau*), ridge
cribin, serrated ridge
crug (pl *crugiau*), mound
cul, narrow
cwm, valley, corrie
cyrn, peak

dan, under
darren, hill
ddu, black
ddŵr, water
ddysgl, dish
deg, beautiful
deu, two
diffwys, precipice
din (*dinas*), fort
dir, land
draeth, beach
draws, across
dref, hamlet, home
drum, ridge

drws, pass
dwr (*dŵr*), water
dwy, two
dyffryn, valley

eglwys, church
eira, snow
eryr, eagle
esgair, ridge

fach, small
fan, place, high place
fawr, large
fechan, small
felin, mill
ffordd, road
ffridd (*ffrith*), hillside pasture
ffrwd, waterfall
ffynnon, spring, well
foel, bare hill
fraith, speckled, pied, variegated
fras, prominent
fron, rounded hill

gader (*gadair*), chair, fortress
gaer, fort
gallt, hillside
gardd, garden
garn, rock
garth, hill
glan, bank
glas (pl *gleision*), green, blue
glyder, heap
glyn, glen
gors, bog
gribin, serrated ridge
grisiau, steps
grug, heather
gwen, white
gwydd, woodland
gwyn, white
gwynt, wind

hafod (*hafoty*), summer dwelling
haul, sun
hen, old
hendre, winter dwelling
heol, road
hir (pl *hirion*), long
hyll, ugly

isaf, lowest

lan, bank
llan, church, village
llawr, flat valley bottom
llech, slate
llechog, slaty
llechwedd, hillside
llwyd, grey
llyn (pl *llynnoedd* or *llynnau*), lake
llys, court

maen, stone
maes, field
man, high place
mawn, peat
mawr, large
melin, mill
melyn, yellow
migyn (*mign*), bog
moch, pigs
moel, bare hill
mur (pl *muriau*), wall
mwyn, mineral, ore
mynydd, mountain

nadroedd, snakes
nant, stream, valley
neuadd, hall
newydd, new

ochr, side
oer, cold
ogof, cave

parc, field, park
pen, top
penrhyn, headland
pentref (pentre), village
person, parson
pistyll, waterfall
plas, mansion
pont, bridge
pwll, pit, pool

rhaeadr, waterfall
rhedyn, bracken
rhiw, hill
rhos, marsh, moor
rhyd, ford

saeth (pl. *saethau*), arrow
sych, dry
teyrn, king
tir, land
traeth, shore
traws, across
tref, hamlet, home
tri, three
trum, ridge
twll, hole
tŵr, tower
tŷ, house
tyddyn, smallholding

uchaf, highest
uwch, above

waun (waen), moor
wen, white
wrach, witch
wyddfa, burial mound, viewpoint

y, the, of the
yn, in
ynys, island, riverside meadow
yr, the, of the
ystrad, valley floor

Bibliography

Addison, K., *Snowdon in the Ice Age*, 1988

Ashton, S., *The Ridges of Snowdonia*, 1985

Barber, C., *The Romance of the Welsh Mountains*, 1986

Bick, D.E., *The Old Copper Mines on Snowdonia*, 1982

Borrow, G., *Wild Wales*, 1862

Carr, H.R.C. & Lister, G.A., *The Mountains of Snowdonia*, 1925

Condry, W., *The Snowdonia National Park*, 1966

Hoare, D.L.F., *Snowdon*, 1987

Hall, V., *A Scrapbook of Snowdonia*, 1982

Howells, M.F., Leveridge, B.E., Reedman, A.J., *Snowdonia*, 1981

Jenkins, J.G., *Life & Tradition in Rural Wales*, 1976

Jones, J., *The Lakes of North Wales*, 1983

North, F.J., Campbell, B., Scott, R., *Snowdonia*, 1949

North Wales Wildlife Trust, *The Nature of North Wales*, 1989

Poucher, W.A., *The Welsh Peaks*, 1962

Readhead, B., *The National Parks of England & Wales*, 1988

Styles, S., *The Mountains of North Wales*, 1973

Turner, K., *The Snowdon Mountain Railway*, 1973

Williams, P., *Rock Climbing in Snowdonia*, 1990

Williams, R., *Three Stops to the Summit*, 1990

Index